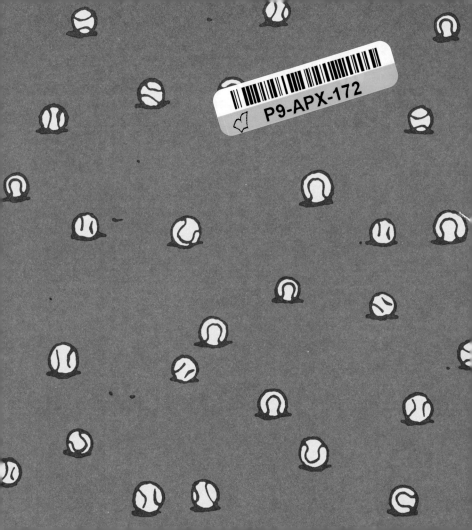

P9-APX-172

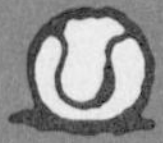

Batter Up, Charlie Brown!

CHARLES M. SCHULZ

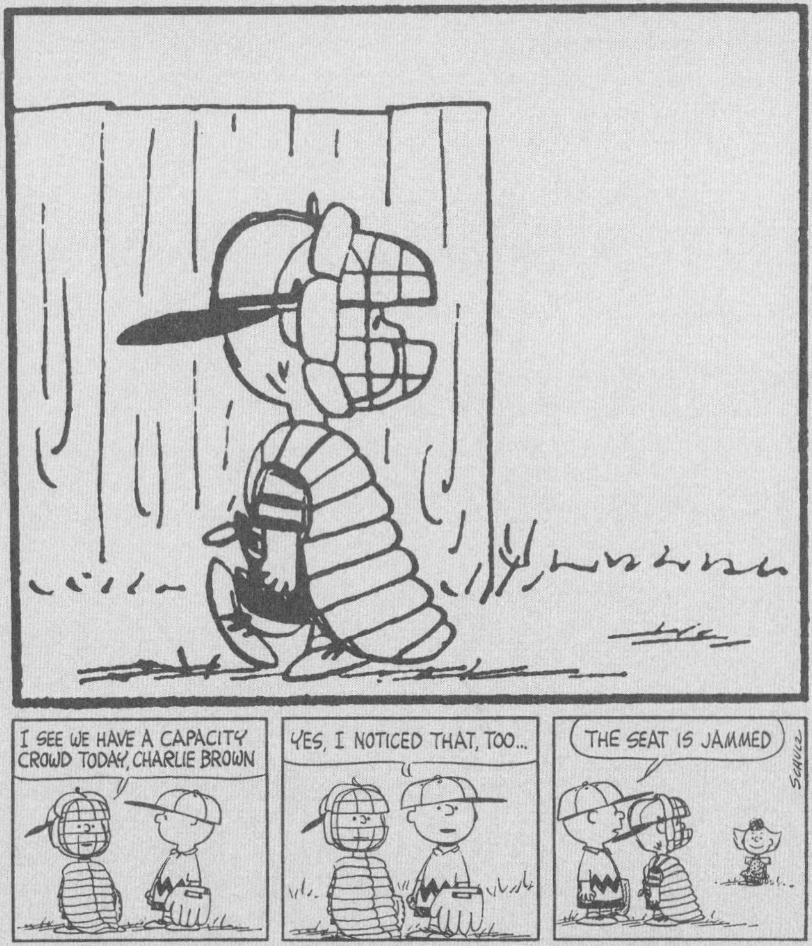
I SEE WE HAVE A CAPACITY CROWD TODAY, CHARLIE BROWN
YES, I NOTICED THAT, TOO...
THE SEAT IS JAMMED
SCHULZ

MANAGER

BATTER UP!

SLIDE!

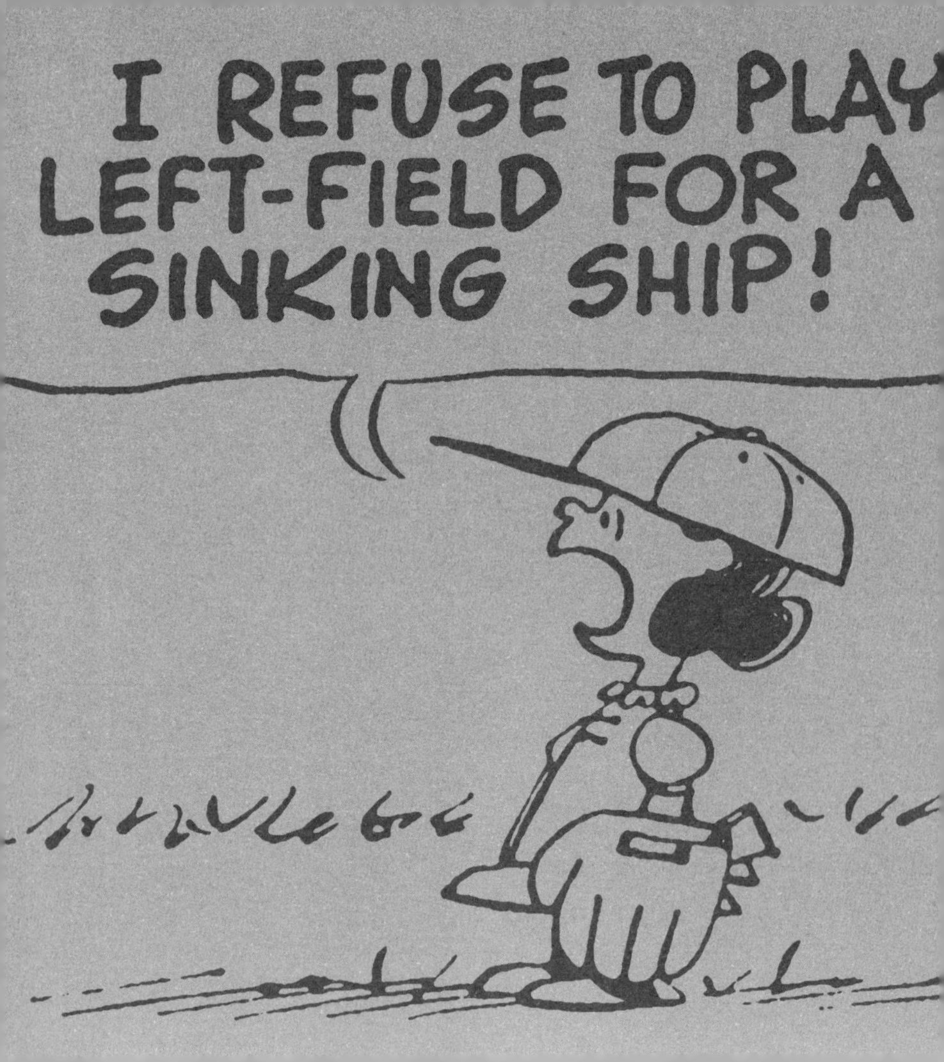
I REFUSE TO PLAY LEFT-FIELD FOR A SINKING SHIP!

X

"TEAM MANAGER"

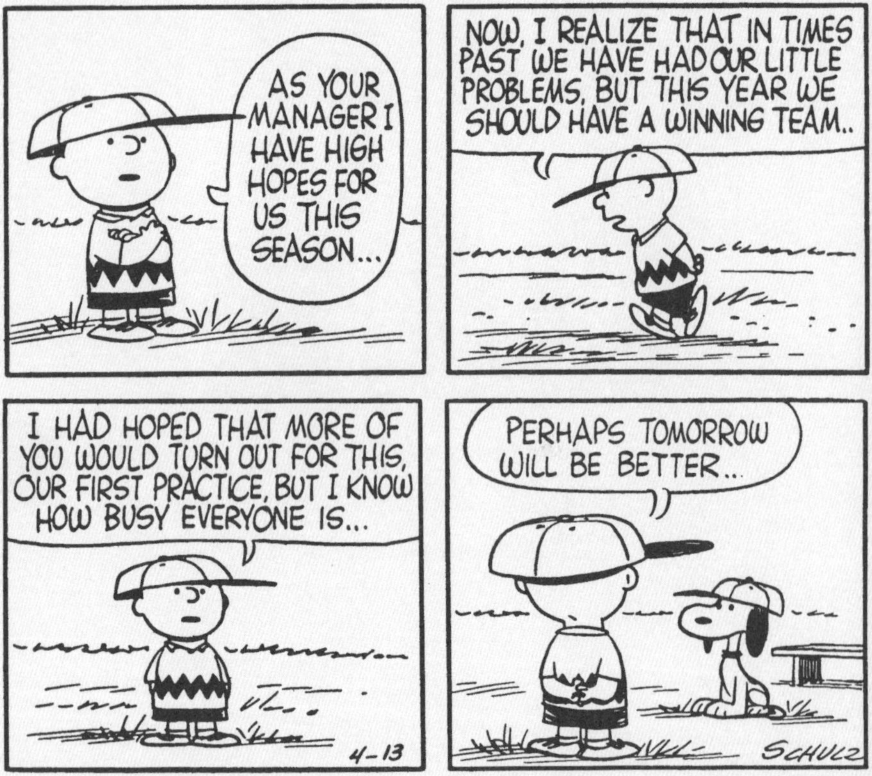
AS YOUR MANAGER I HAVE HIGH HOPES FOR US THIS SEASON...
NOW, I REALIZE THAT IN TIMES PAST WE HAVE HAD OUR LITTLE PROBLEMS, BUT THIS YEAR WE SHOULD HAVE A WINNING TEAM..
I HAD HOPED THAT MORE OF YOU WOULD TURN OUT FOR THIS, OUR FIRST PRACTICE, BUT I KNOW HOW BUSY EVERYONE IS...
4-13
PERHAPS TOMORROW WILL BE BETTER...
SCHULZ

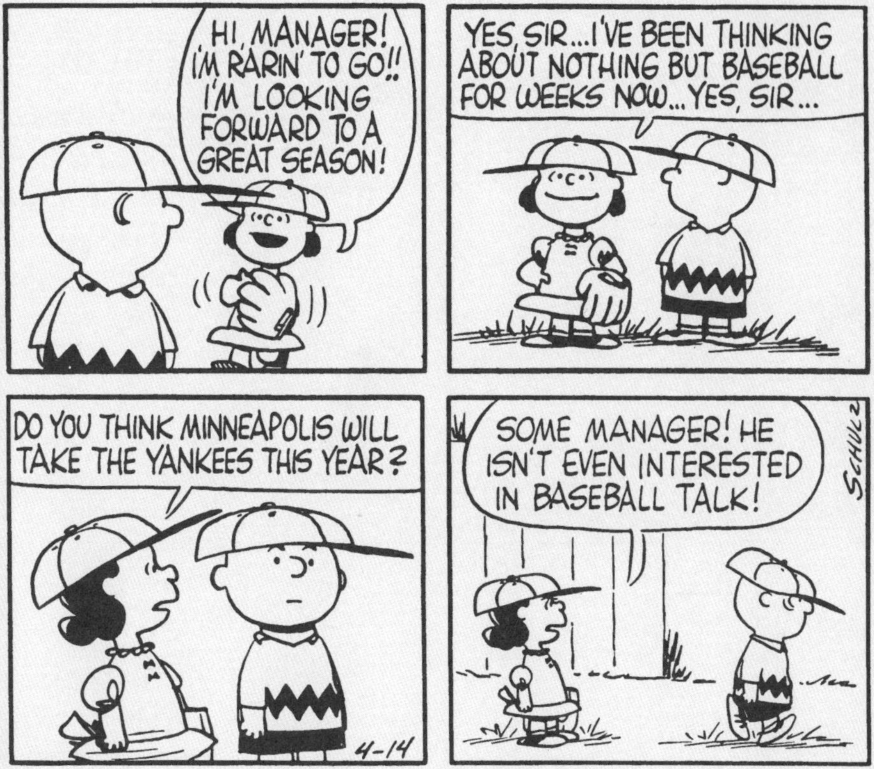
HI, MANAGER! I'M RARIN' TO GO!! I'M LOOKING FORWARD TO A GREAT SEASON!
YES, SIR...I'VE BEEN THINKING ABOUT NOTHING BUT BASEBALL FOR WEEKS NOW...YES, SIR...
DO YOU THINK MINNEAPOLIS WILL TAKE THE YANKEES THIS YEAR?
4-14
SOME MANAGER! HE ISN'T EVEN INTERESTED IN BASEBALL TALK!
SCHULZ

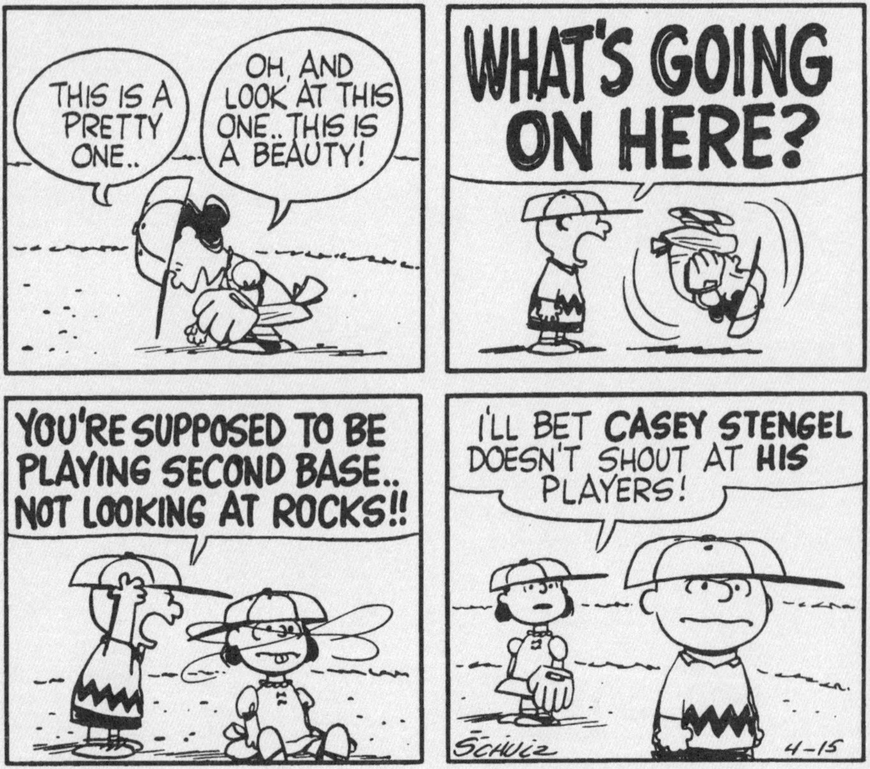
THIS IS A PRETTY ONE..
OH, AND LOOK AT THIS ONE.. THIS IS A BEAUTY!
WHAT'S GOING ON HERE?
YOU'RE SUPPOSED TO BE PLAYING SECOND BASE.. NOT LOOKING AT ROCKS!!
I'LL BET CASEY STENGEL DOESN'T SHOUT AT HIS PLAYERS!
SCHULZ
4-15

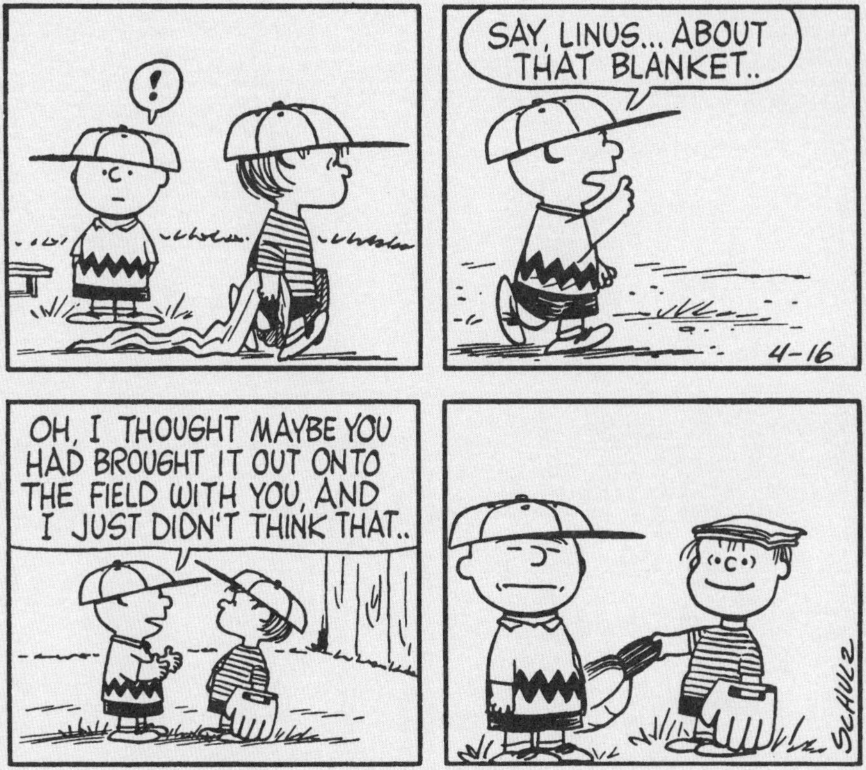
!
SAY, LINUS... ABOUT THAT BLANKET..
4-16
OH, I THOUGHT MAYBE YOU HAD BROUGHT IT OUT ONTO THE FIELD WITH YOU, AND I JUST DIDN'T THINK THAT..
SCHULZ

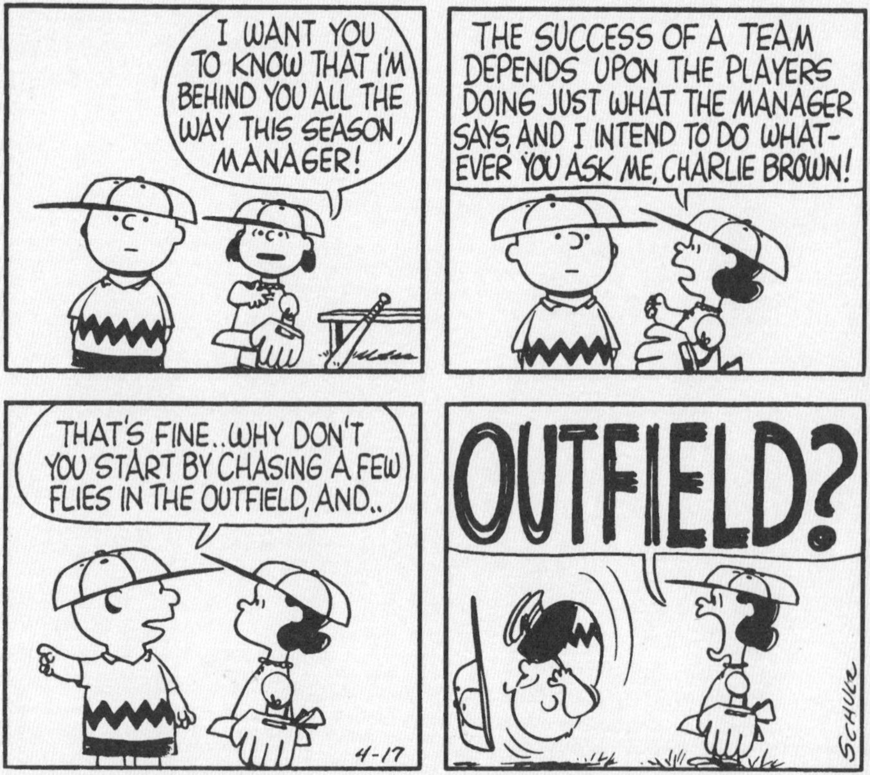
I WANT YOU TO KNOW THAT I'M BEHIND YOU ALL THE WAY THIS SEASON, MANAGER!
THE SUCCESS OF A TEAM DEPENDS UPON THE PLAYERS DOING JUST WHAT THE MANAGER SAYS, AND I INTEND TO DO WHATEVER YOU ASK ME, CHARLIE BROWN!
THAT'S FINE..WHY DON'T YOU START BY CHASING A FEW FLIES IN THE OUTFIELD, AND..
OUTFIELD?
4-17
SCHULZ

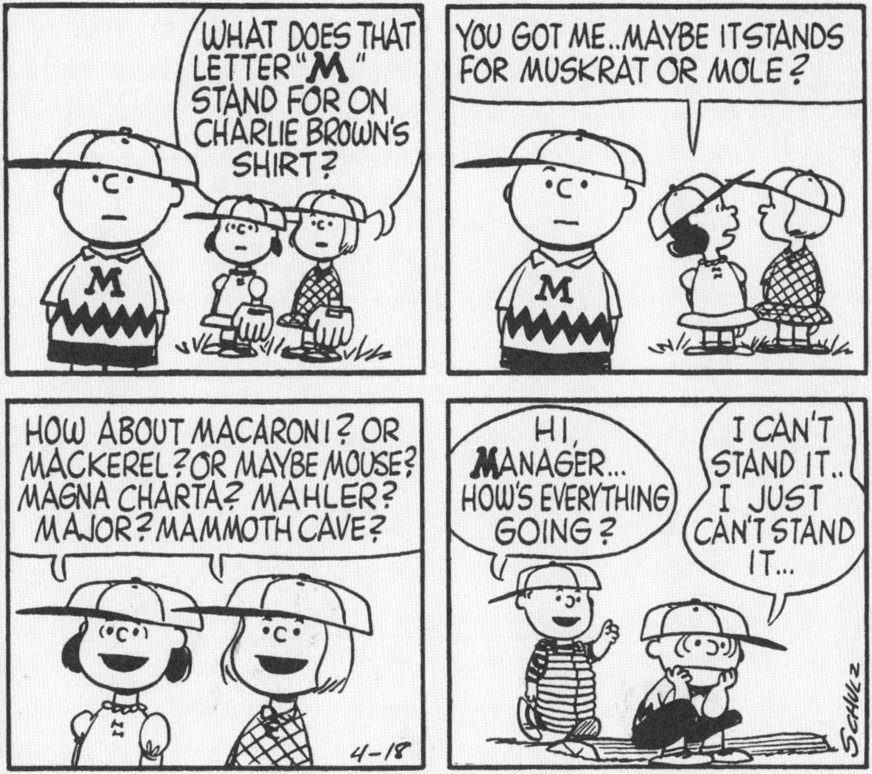
WHAT DOES THAT LETTER "M" STAND FOR ON CHARLIE BROWN'S SHIRT?
YOU GOT ME..MAYBE IT STANDS FOR MUSKRAT OR MOLE?
HOW ABOUT MACARONI? OR MACKEREL? OR MAYBE MOUSE? MAGNA CHARTA? MAHLER? MAJOR? MAMMOTH CAVE?
4-18
HI, MANAGER... HOW'S EVERYTHING GOING?
I CAN'T STAND IT.. I JUST CAN'T STAND IT...
SCHULZ

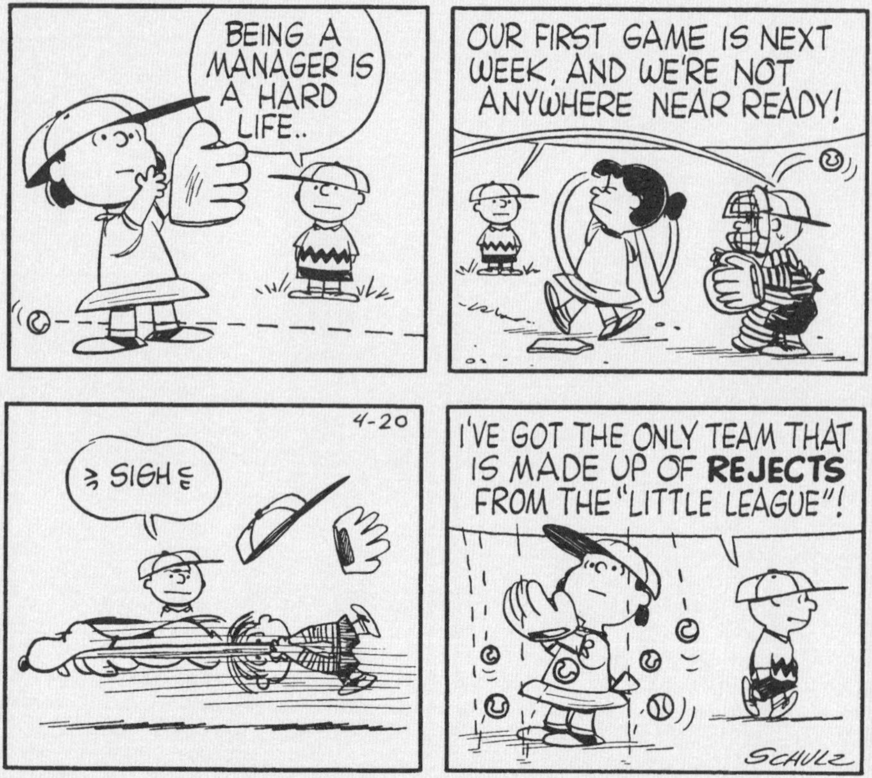
BEING A MANAGER IS A HARD LIFE..
OUR FIRST GAME IS NEXT WEEK, AND WE'RE NOT ANYWHERE NEAR READY!
4-20
SIGH
I'VE GOT THE ONLY TEAM THAT IS MADE UP OF **REJECTS** FROM THE "LITTLE LEAGUE"!
SCHULZ

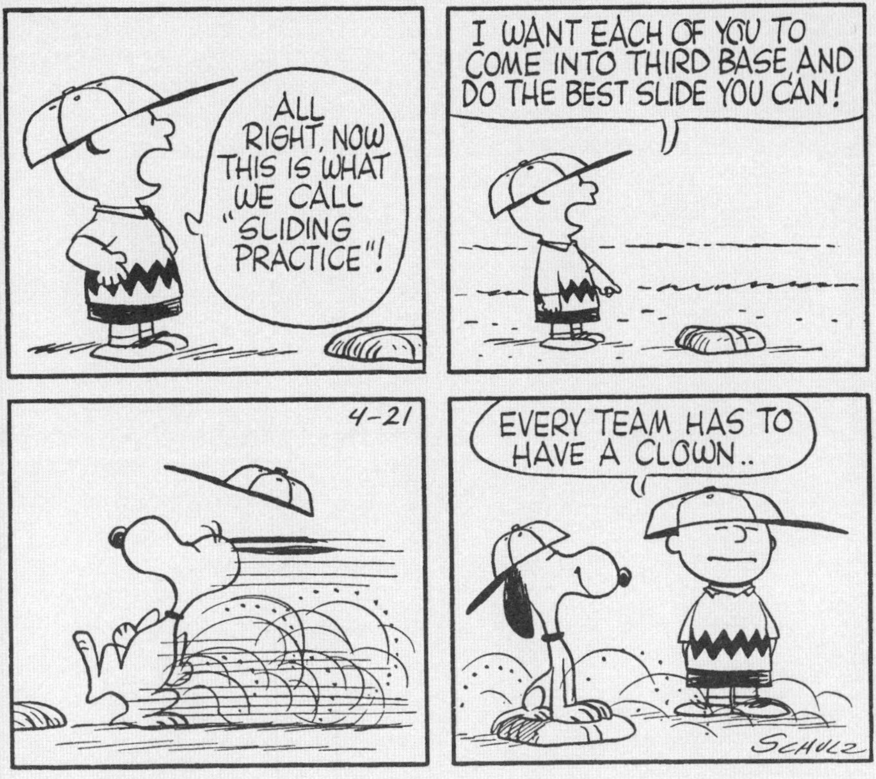
ALL RIGHT, NOW THIS IS WHAT WE CALL "SLIDING PRACTICE"!
I WANT EACH OF YOU TO COME INTO THIRD BASE, AND DO THE BEST SLIDE YOU CAN!
4-21
EVERY TEAM HAS TO HAVE A CLOWN..
SCHULZ

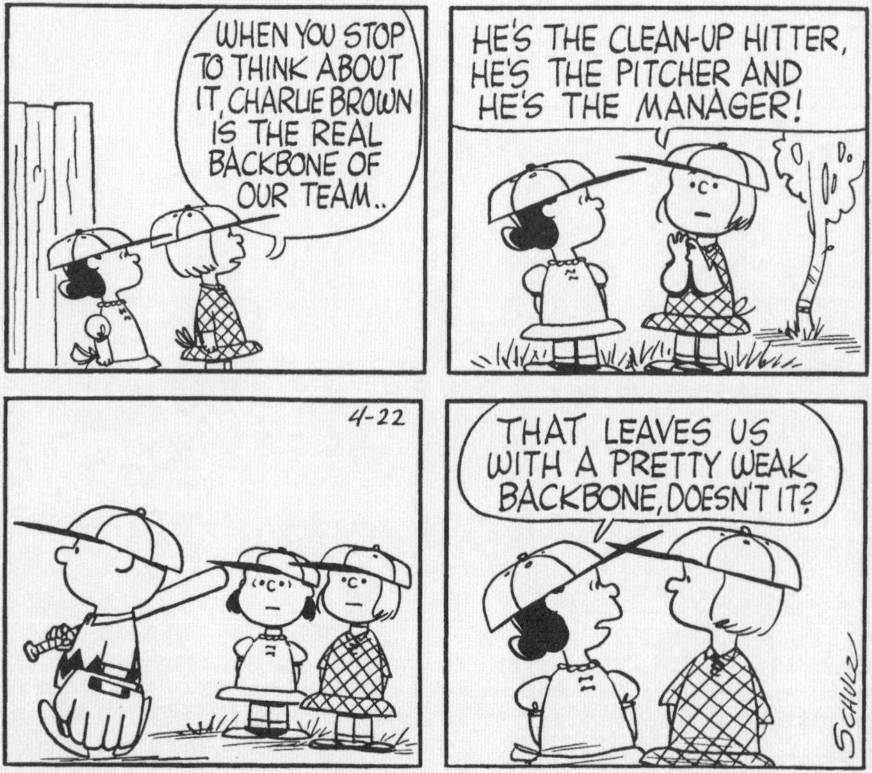
WHEN YOU STOP TO THINK ABOUT IT, CHARLIE BROWN IS THE REAL BACKBONE OF OUR TEAM..
HE'S THE CLEAN-UP HITTER, HE'S THE PITCHER AND HE'S THE MANAGER!
4-22
THAT LEAVES US WITH A PRETTY WEAK BACKBONE, DOESN'T IT?
SCHULZ

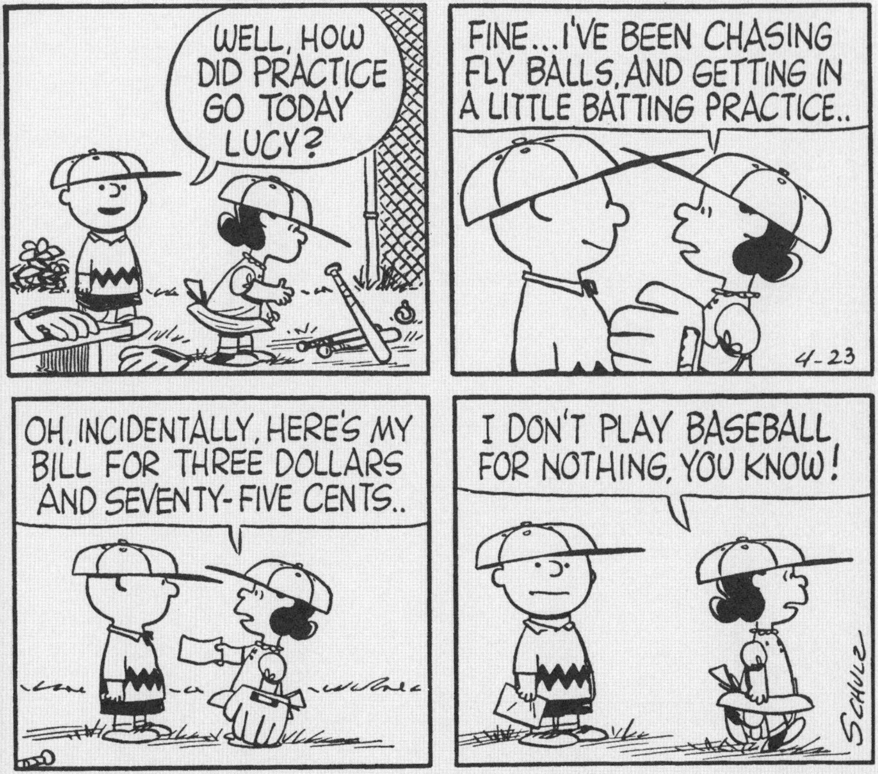
WELL, HOW DID PRACTICE GO TODAY LUCY?
FINE...I'VE BEEN CHASING FLY BALLS, AND GETTING IN A LITTLE BATTING PRACTICE..
4-23
OH, INCIDENTALLY, HERE'S MY BILL FOR THREE DOLLARS AND SEVENTY-FIVE CENTS..
I DON'T PLAY BASEBALL FOR NOTHING, YOU KNOW!
SCHULZ

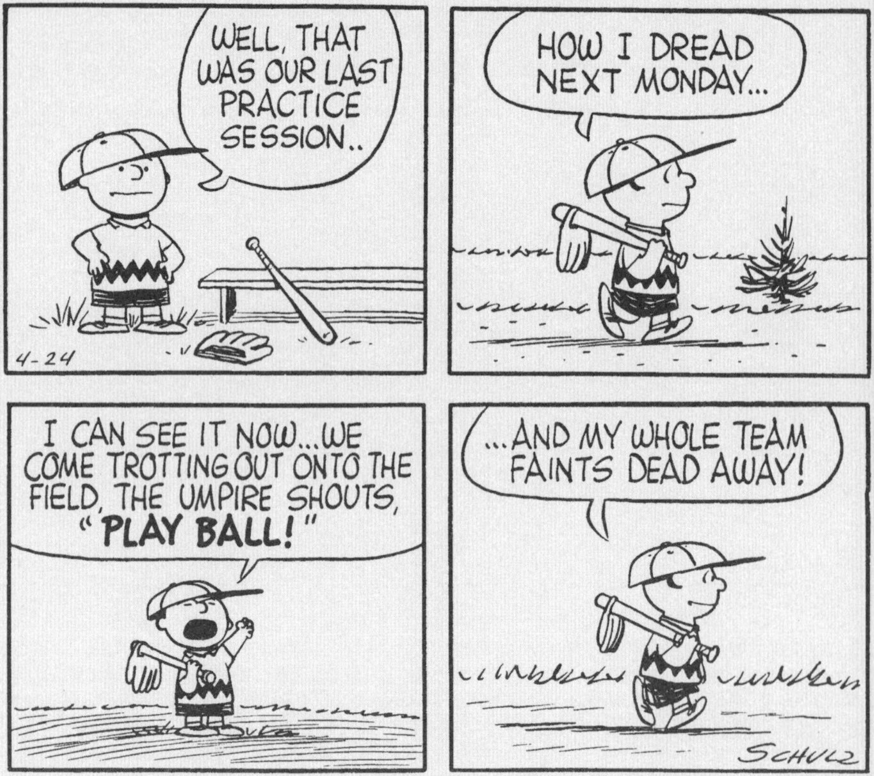
WELL, THAT WAS OUR LAST PRACTICE SESSION..
4-24
HOW I DREAD NEXT MONDAY...
I CAN SEE IT NOW...WE COME TROTTING OUT ONTO THE FIELD, THE UMPIRE SHOUTS, "PLAY BALL!"
...AND MY WHOLE TEAM FAINTS DEAD AWAY!
SCHULZ

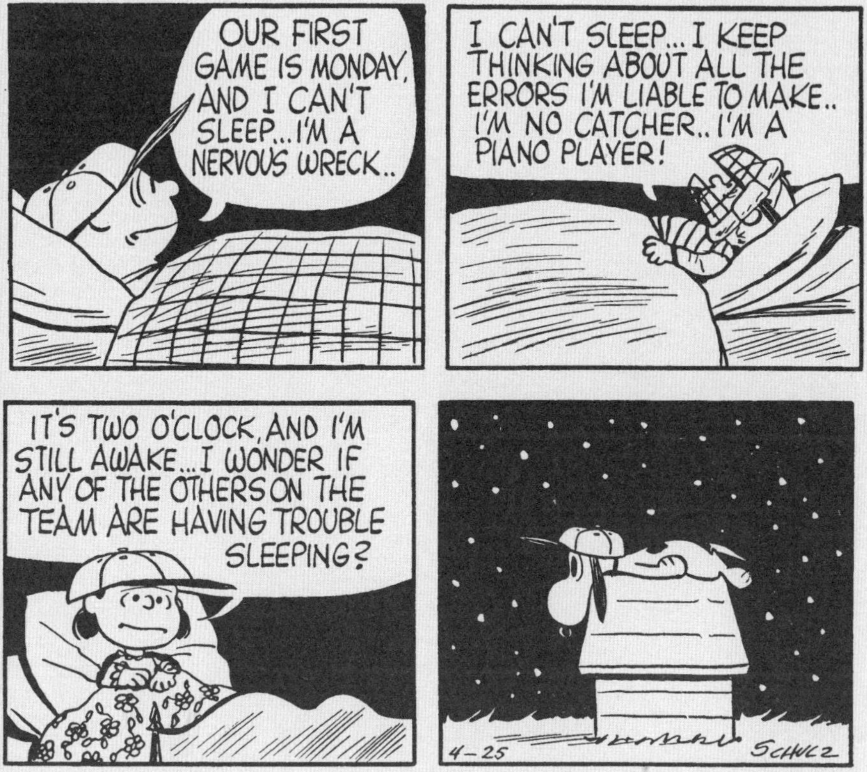
OUR FIRST GAME IS MONDAY, AND I CAN'T SLEEP... I'M A NERVOUS WRECK..
I CAN'T SLEEP... I KEEP THINKING ABOUT ALL THE ERRORS I'M LIABLE TO MAKE.. I'M NO CATCHER.. I'M A PIANO PLAYER!
IT'S TWO O'CLOCK, AND I'M STILL AWAKE... I WONDER IF ANY OF THE OTHERS ON THE TEAM ARE HAVING TROUBLE SLEEPING?
4-25
SCHULZ

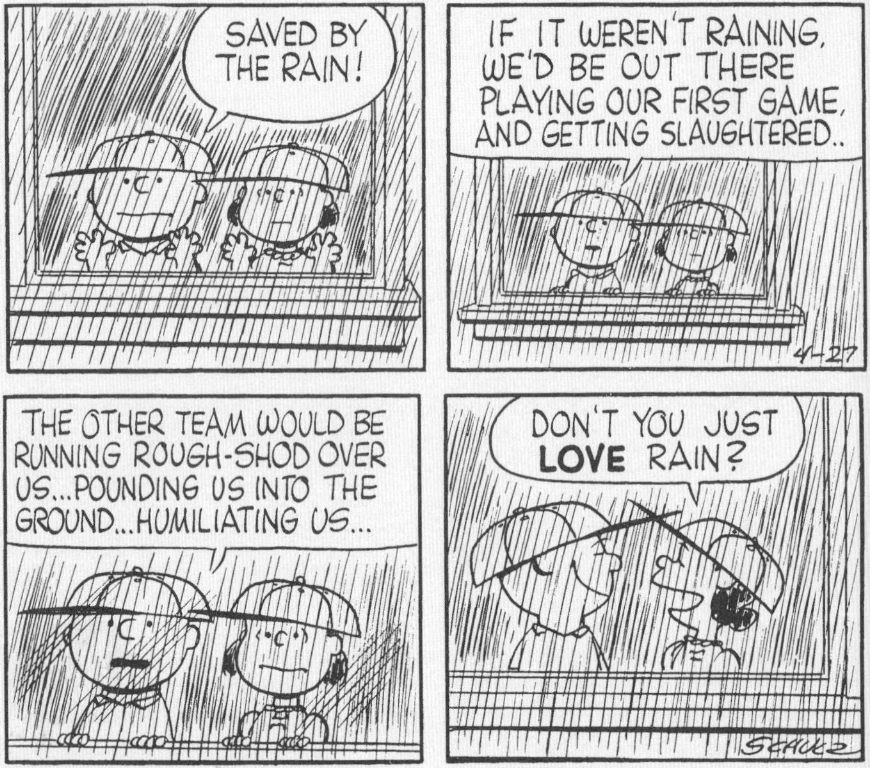
SAVED BY THE RAIN!
IF IT WEREN'T RAINING, WE'D BE OUT THERE PLAYING OUR FIRST GAME, AND GETTING SLAUGHTERED..
4-27
THE OTHER TEAM WOULD BE RUNNING ROUGH-SHOD OVER US...POUNDING US INTO THE GROUND...HUMILIATING US...
DON'T YOU JUST **LOVE** RAIN?
SCHULZ

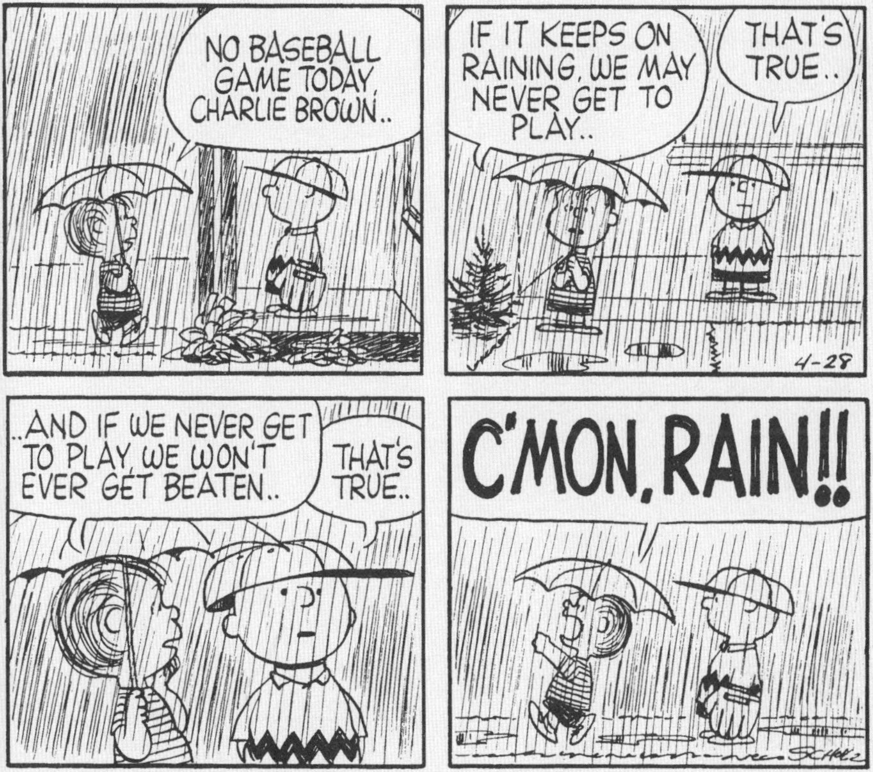
NO BASEBALL GAME TODAY, CHARLIE BROWN..
IF IT KEEPS ON RAINING, WE MAY NEVER GET TO PLAY..
THAT'S TRUE..
4-28
..AND IF WE NEVER GET TO PLAY, WE WON'T EVER GET BEATEN..
THAT'S TRUE..
C'MON, RAIN!!
SCHULZ

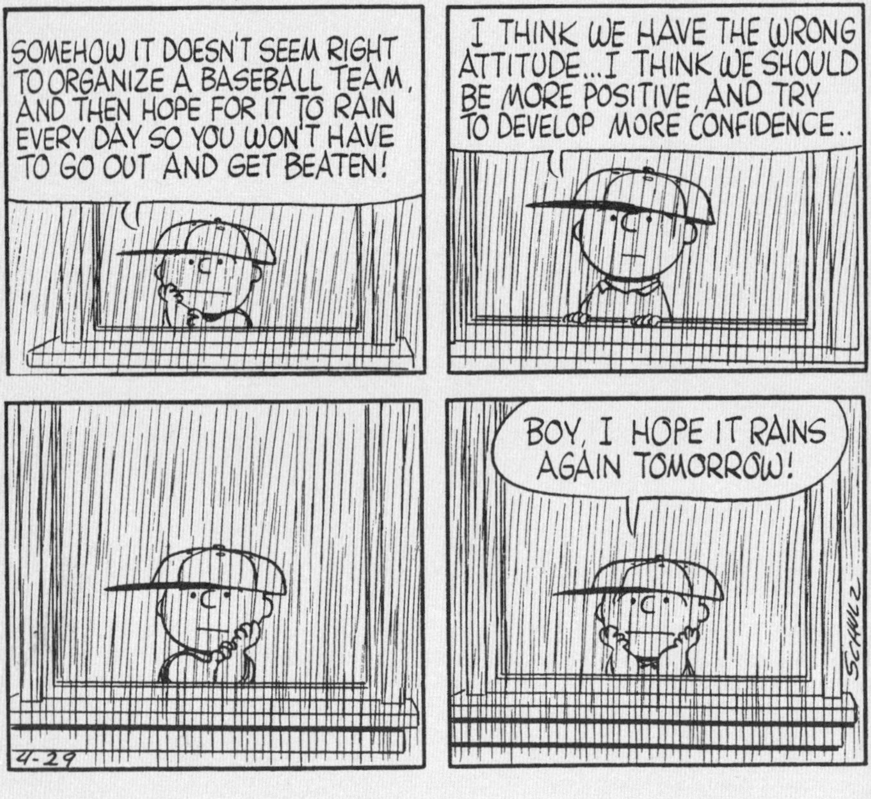
SOMEHOW IT DOESN'T SEEM RIGHT TO ORGANIZE A BASEBALL TEAM, AND THEN HOPE FOR IT TO RAIN EVERY DAY SO YOU WON'T HAVE TO GO OUT AND GET BEATEN!
I THINK WE HAVE THE WRONG ATTITUDE...I THINK WE SHOULD BE MORE POSITIVE, AND TRY TO DEVELOP MORE CONFIDENCE..
4-29
BOY, I HOPE IT RAINS AGAIN TOMORROW!
SCHULZ

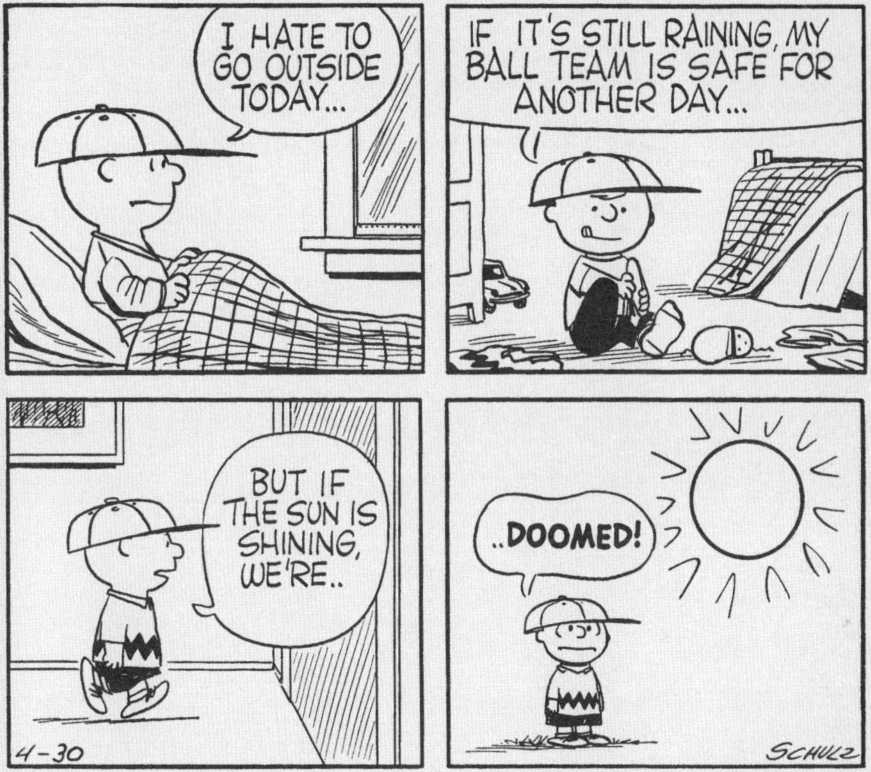
I HATE TO GO OUTSIDE TODAY...
IF IT'S STILL RAINING, MY BALL TEAM IS SAFE FOR ANOTHER DAY...
BUT IF THE SUN IS SHINING, WE'RE..
..DOOMED!
4-30
SCHULZ

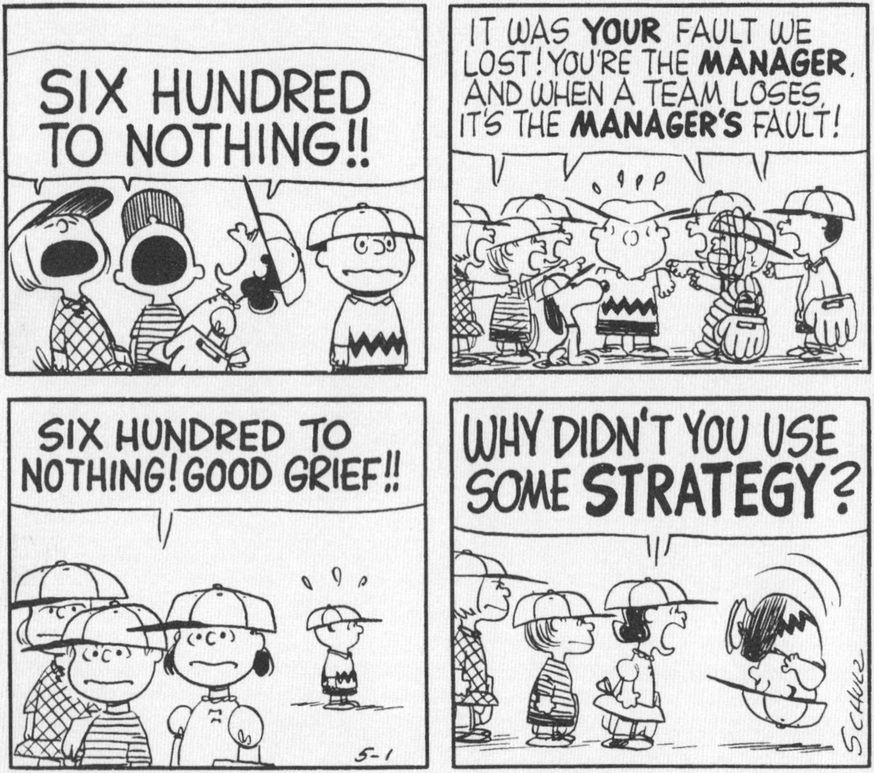
SIX HUNDRED TO NOTHING!!
IT WAS **YOUR** FAULT WE LOST! YOU'RE THE **MANAGER**, AND WHEN A TEAM LOSES, IT'S THE **MANAGER'S** FAULT!
SIX HUNDRED TO NOTHING! GOOD GRIEF!!
5-1
WHY DIDN'T YOU USE SOME STRATEGY?
SCHULZ

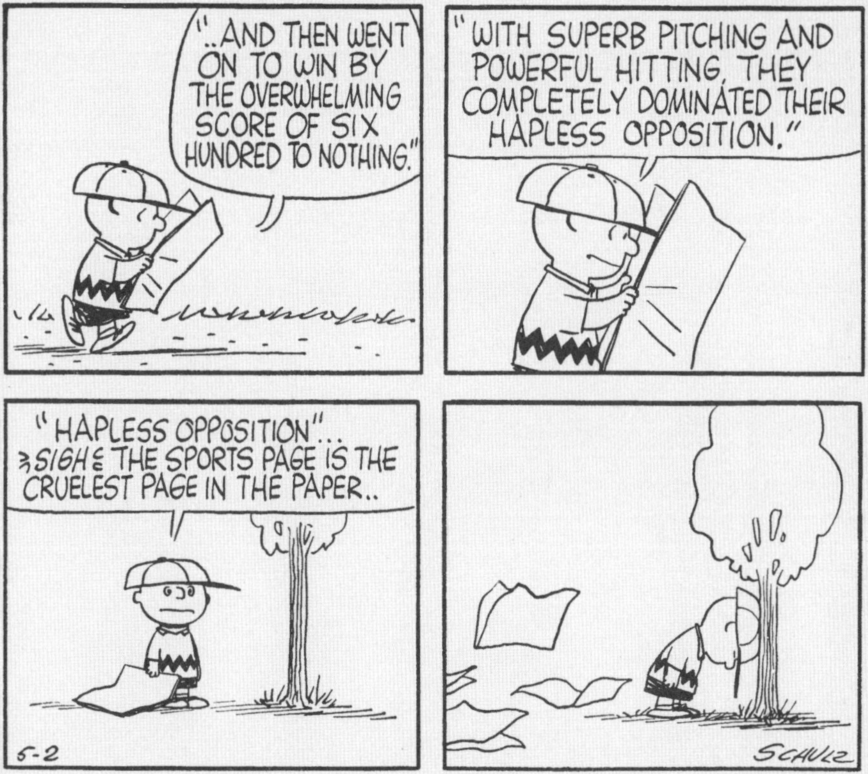
"..AND THEN WENT ON TO WIN BY THE OVERWHELMING SCORE OF SIX HUNDRED TO NOTHING."
"WITH SUPERB PITCHING AND POWERFUL HITTING, THEY COMPLETELY DOMINATED THEIR HAPLESS OPPOSITION."
"HAPLESS OPPOSITION"... SIGH THE SPORTS PAGE IS THE CRUELEST PAGE IN THE PAPER..
5-2
SCHULZ

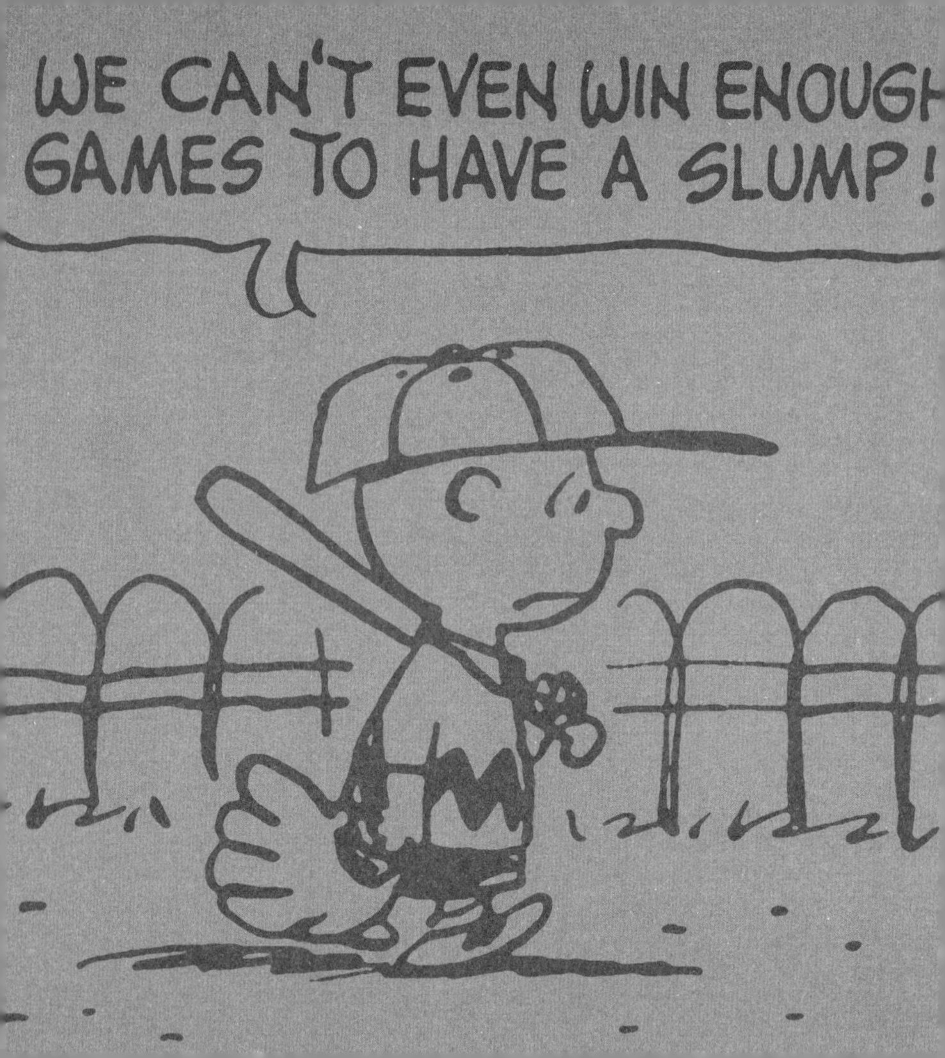
WE CAN'T EVEN WIN ENOUGH GAMES TO HAVE A SLUMP!

XX

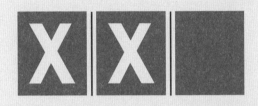

“BATTER UP!”

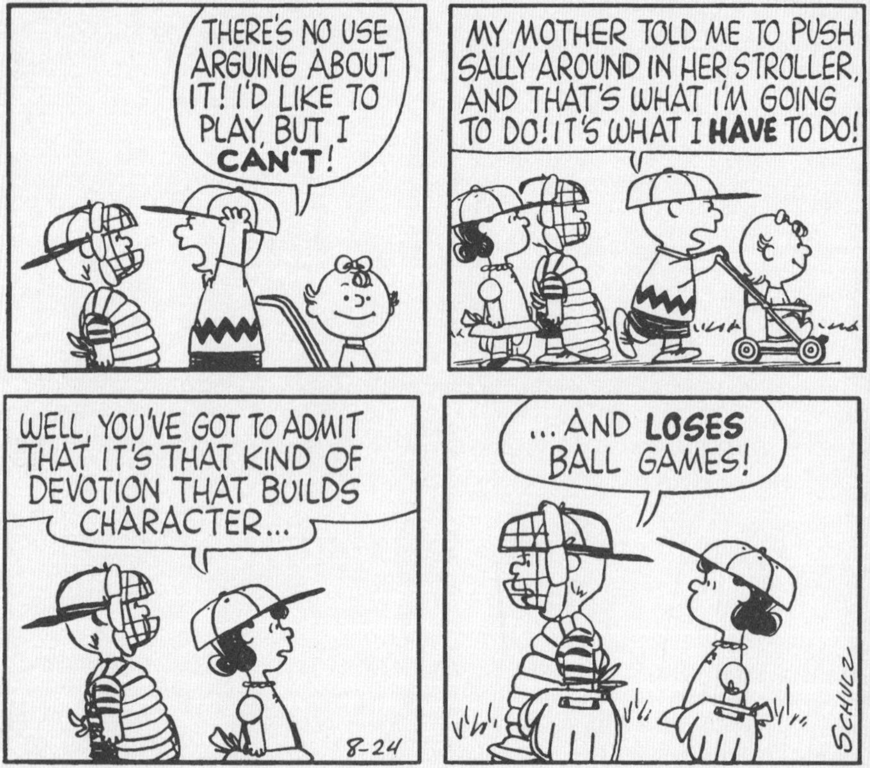
THERE'S NO USE ARGUING ABOUT IT! I'D LIKE TO PLAY, BUT I **CAN'T**!
MY MOTHER TOLD ME TO PUSH SALLY AROUND IN HER STROLLER, AND THAT'S WHAT I'M GOING TO DO! IT'S WHAT I **HAVE** TO DO!
WELL, YOU'VE GOT TO ADMIT THAT IT'S THAT KIND OF DEVOTION THAT BUILDS CHARACTER...
8-24
...AND **LOSES** BALL GAMES!
SCHULZ

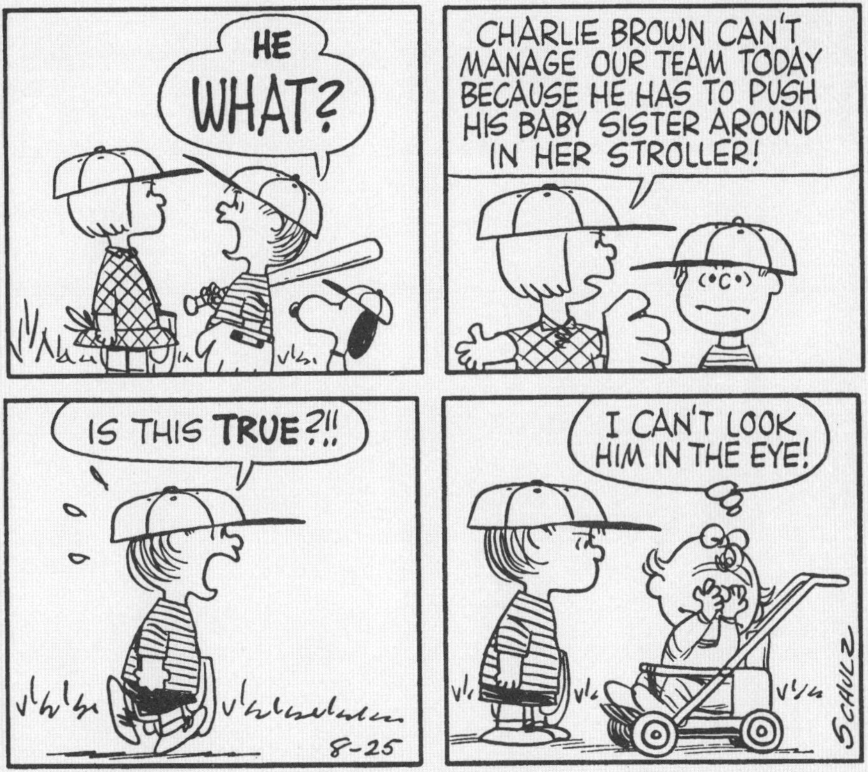
HE WHAT?
CHARLIE BROWN CAN'T MANAGE OUR TEAM TODAY BECAUSE HE HAS TO PUSH HIS BABY SISTER AROUND IN HER STROLLER!
IS THIS TRUE?!!
8-25
I CAN'T LOOK HIM IN THE EYE!
SCHULZ

I HOPE SHE'S **SATISFIED**!
DEPRIVING US OF A MANAGER JUST BEFORE OUR LAST AND MOST CRUCIAL GAME!
8-26
ALL BECAUSE SHE HAS TO RIDE AROUND IN HER OL' STROLLER! **WELL, I JUST HOPE SHE'S SATISFIED!**
MY FIRST YEAR IN THIS WORLD, AND ALREADY I HAVE **GUILT** FEELINGS!
SCHULZ

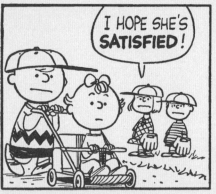

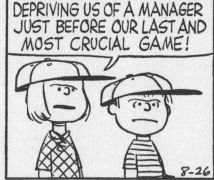

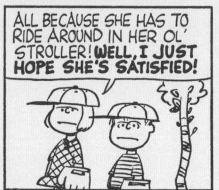

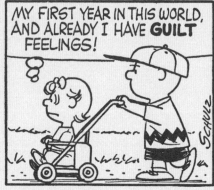

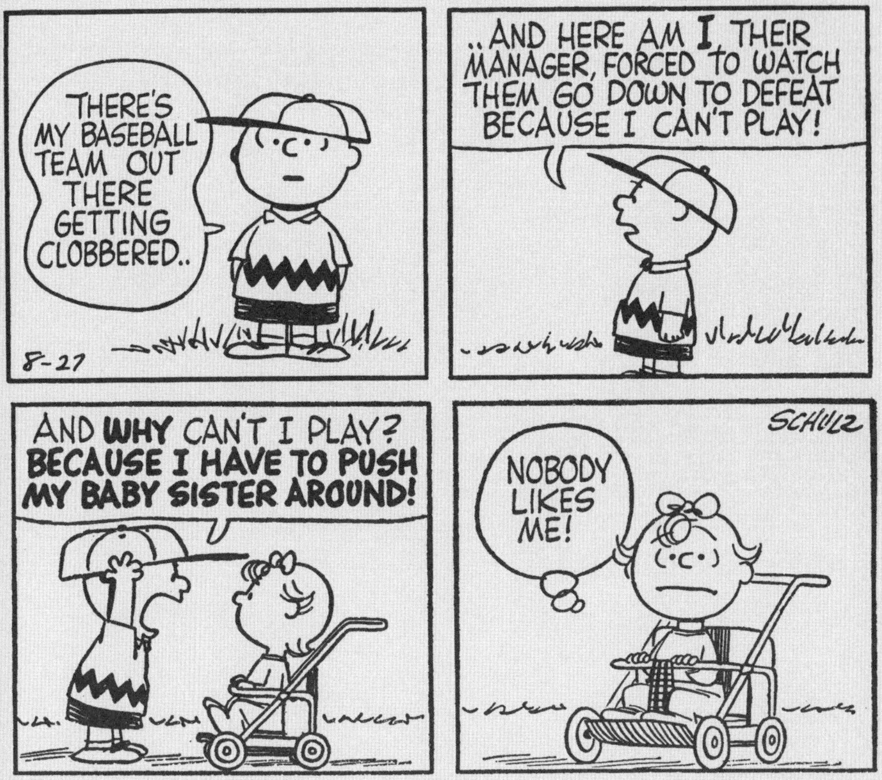
THERE'S MY BASEBALL TEAM OUT THERE GETTING CLOBBERED..
8-27
..AND HERE AM I, THEIR MANAGER, FORCED TO WATCH THEM GO DOWN TO DEFEAT BECAUSE I CAN'T PLAY!
AND WHY CAN'T I PLAY? BECAUSE I HAVE TO PUSH MY BABY SISTER AROUND!
SCHULZ
NOBODY LIKES ME!

HAVE THE INFIELD MOVE IN, AND TRY TO CUT OFF THE RUN AT THE PLATE...

I SHOULD BE BACK HERE IN ABOUT FIVE MINUTES..

GOOD GRIEF!

8-28

I'M THE ONLY MANAGER IN THE HISTORY OF THE GAME TO GUIDE HIS TEAM WHILE PUSHING HIS BABY SISTER AROUND THE BLOCK!

SIGH

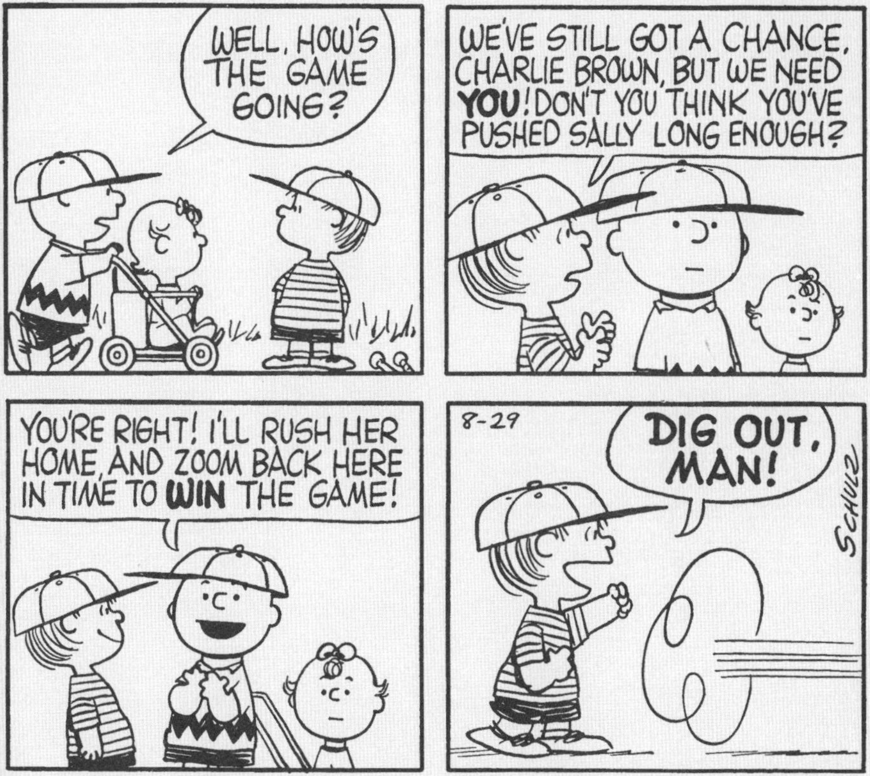
WELL, HOW'S THE GAME GOING?
WE'VE STILL GOT A CHANCE, CHARLIE BROWN, BUT WE NEED YOU! DON'T YOU THINK YOU'VE PUSHED SALLY LONG ENOUGH?
YOU'RE RIGHT! I'LL RUSH HER HOME, AND ZOOM BACK HERE IN TIME TO WIN THE GAME!
8-29
DIG OUT, MAN!
SCHULZ

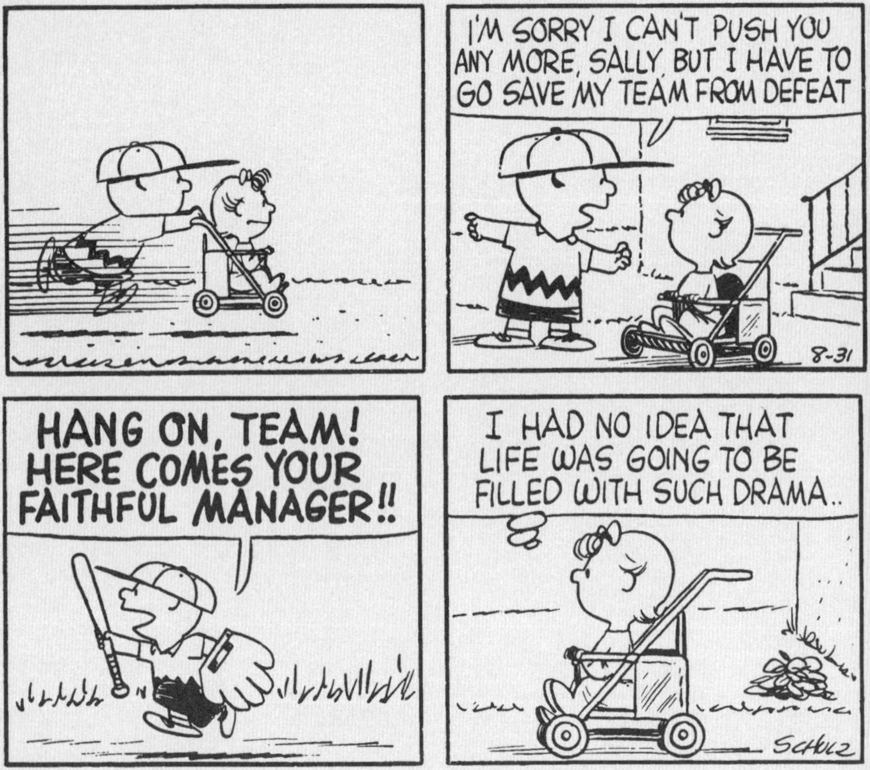
I'M SORRY I CAN'T PUSH YOU ANY MORE, SALLY, BUT I HAVE TO GO SAVE MY TEAM FROM DEFEAT
8-31
HANG ON, TEAM! HERE COMES YOUR FAITHFUL MANAGER!!
I HAD NO IDEA THAT LIFE WAS GOING TO BE FILLED WITH SUCH DRAMA..
SCHULZ

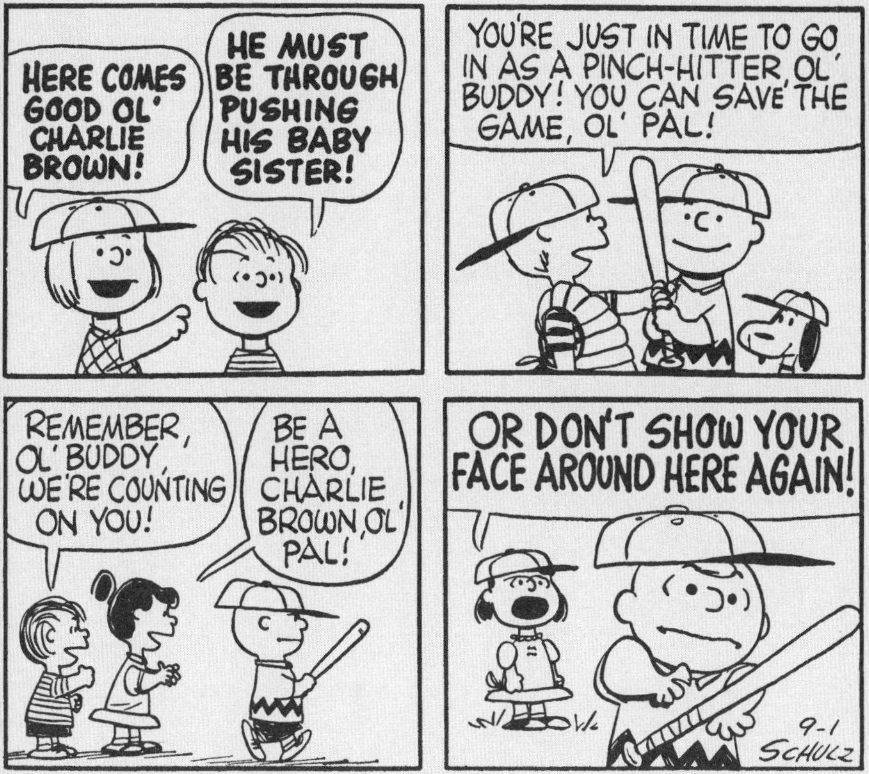
HERE COMES GOOD OL' CHARLIE BROWN!
HE MUST BE THROUGH PUSHING HIS BABY SISTER!
YOU'RE JUST IN TIME TO GO IN AS A PINCH-HITTER, OL' BUDDY! YOU CAN SAVE THE GAME, OL' PAL!
REMEMBER, OL' BUDDY, WE'RE COUNTING ON YOU!
BE A HERO, CHARLIE BROWN, OL' PAL!
OR DON'T SHOW YOUR FACE AROUND HERE AGAIN!
9-1
SCHULZ

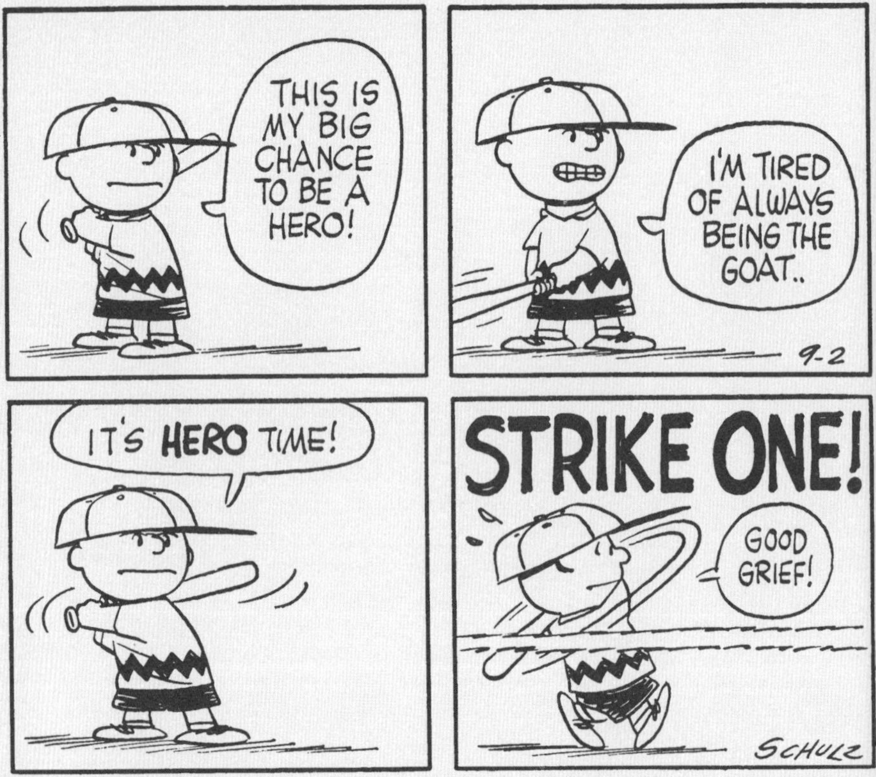
THIS IS MY BIG CHANCE TO BE A HERO!
I'M TIRED OF ALWAYS BEING THE GOAT..
9-2
IT'S **HERO** TIME!
STRIKE ONE!
GOOD GRIEF!
SCHULZ

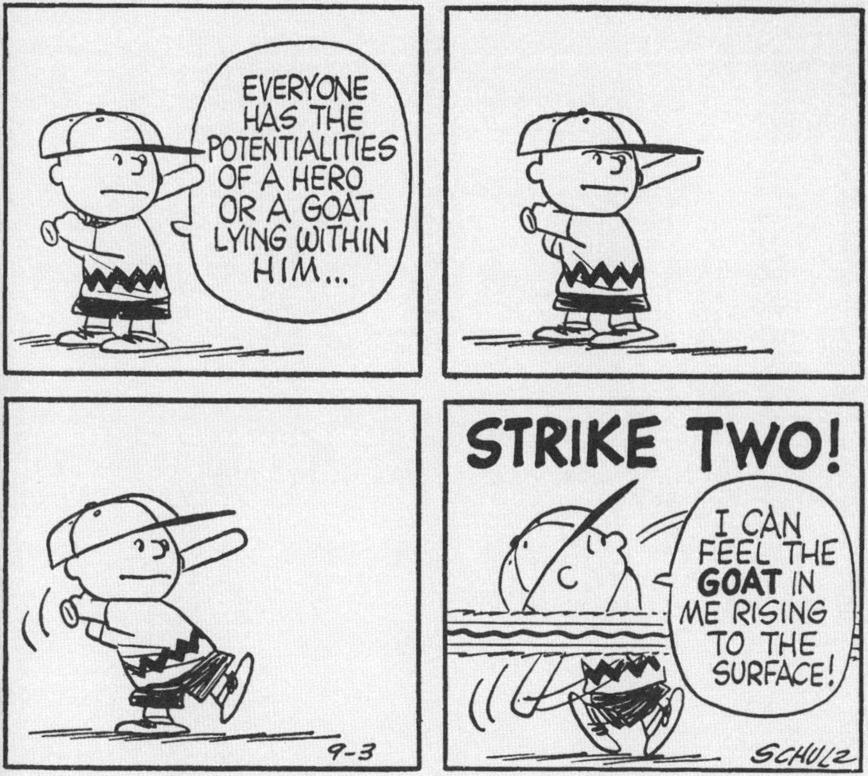
EVERYONE HAS THE POTENTIALITIES OF A HERO OR A GOAT LYING WITHIN HIM...
STRIKE TWO!
I CAN FEEL THE **GOAT** IN ME RISING TO THE SURFACE!
9-3
SCHULZ

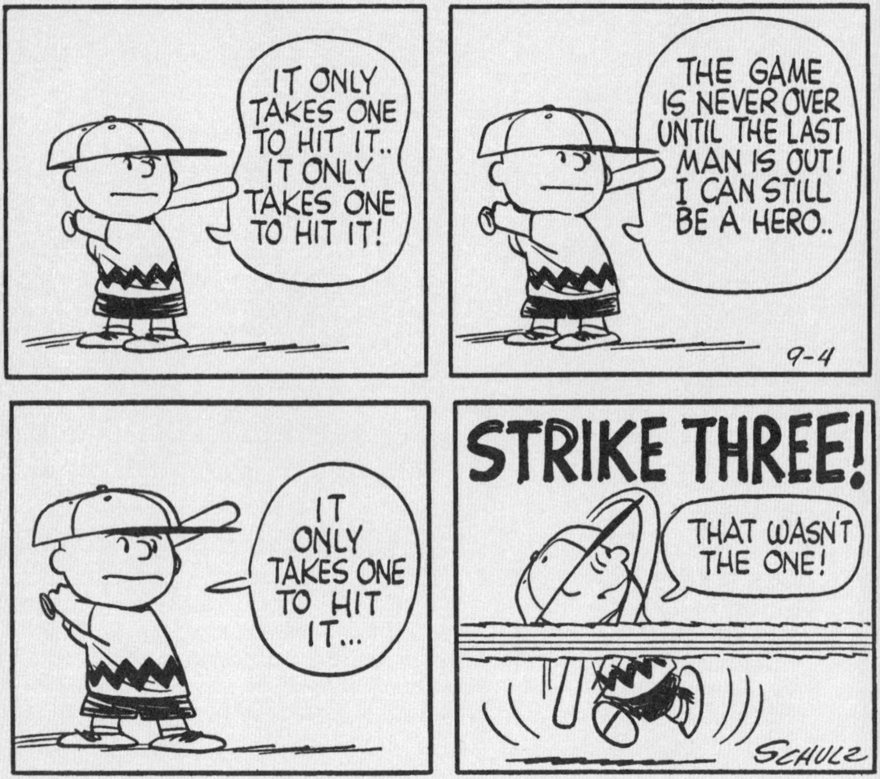
IT ONLY TAKES ONE TO HIT IT.. IT ONLY TAKES ONE TO HIT IT!
THE GAME IS NEVER OVER UNTIL THE LAST MAN IS OUT! I CAN STILL BE A HERO..
9-4
IT ONLY TAKES ONE TO HIT IT...
STRIKE THREE!
THAT WASN'T THE ONE!
SCHULZ

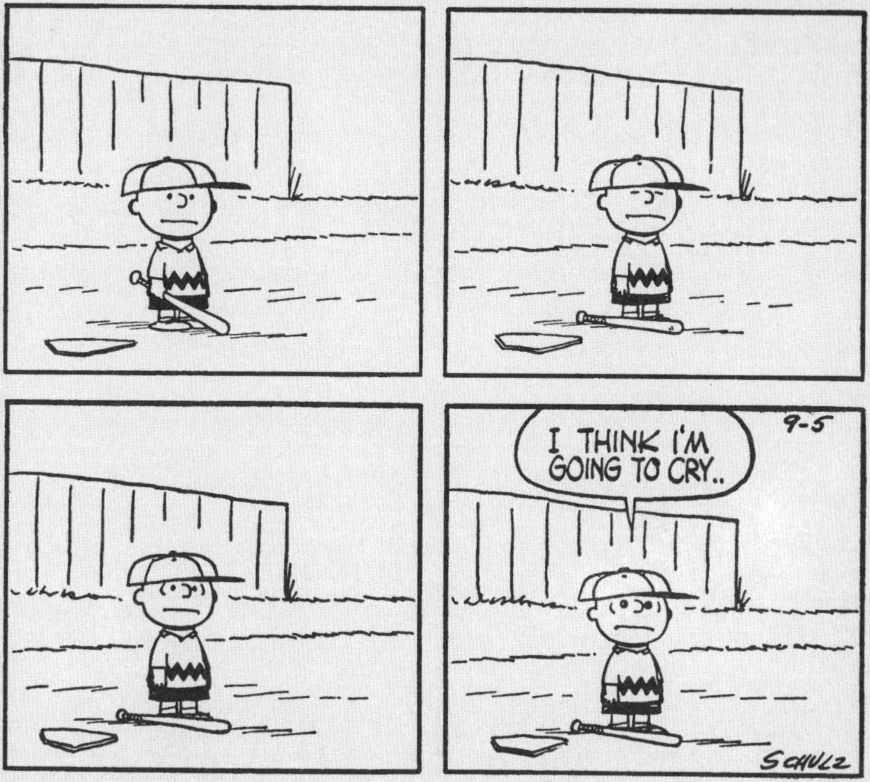
I THINK I'M GOING TO CRY..
9-5
SCHULZ

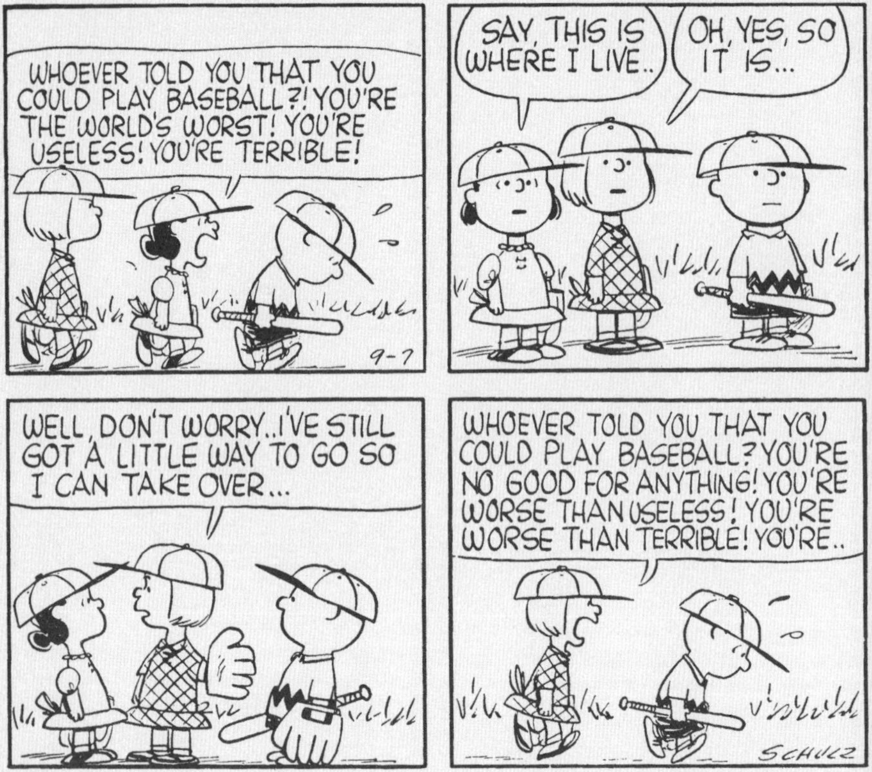
WHOEVER TOLD YOU THAT YOU COULD PLAY BASEBALL?! YOU'RE THE WORLD'S WORST! YOU'RE USELESS! YOU'RE TERRIBLE!
9-7
SAY, THIS IS WHERE I LIVE..
OH, YES, SO IT IS...
WELL, DON'T WORRY..I'VE STILL GOT A LITTLE WAY TO GO SO I CAN TAKE OVER...
WHOEVER TOLD YOU THAT YOU COULD PLAY BASEBALL? YOU'RE NO GOOD FOR ANYTHING! YOU'RE WORSE THAN USELESS! YOU'RE WORSE THAN TERRIBLE! YOU'RE..
SCHULZ

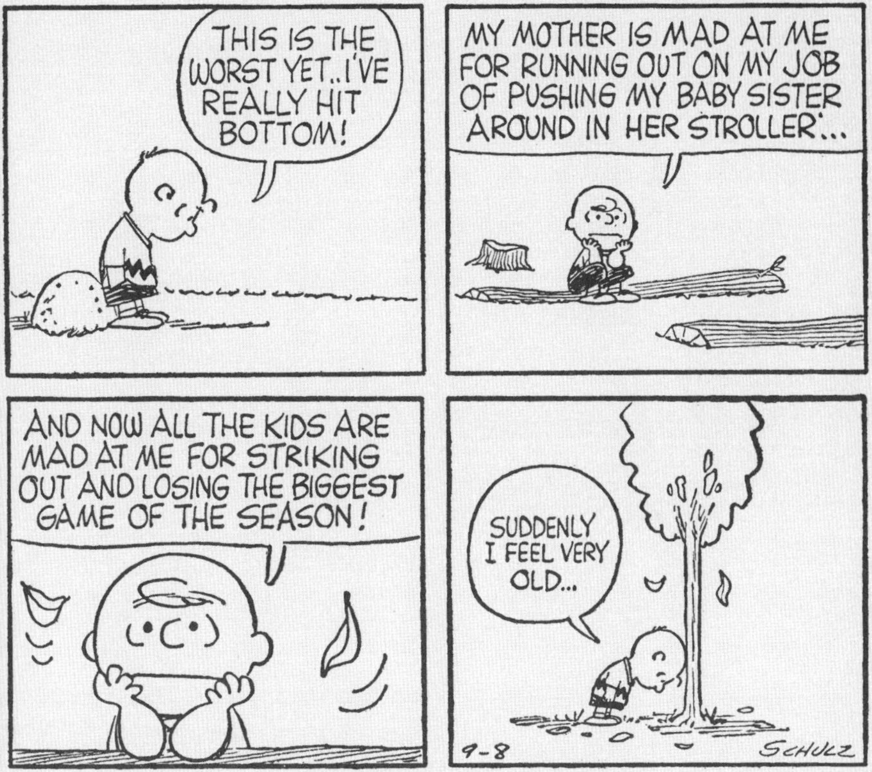
THIS IS THE WORST YET..I'VE REALLY HIT BOTTOM!
MY MOTHER IS MAD AT ME FOR RUNNING OUT ON MY JOB OF PUSHING MY BABY SISTER AROUND IN HER STROLLER...
AND NOW ALL THE KIDS ARE MAD AT ME FOR STRIKING OUT AND LOSING THE BIGGEST GAME OF THE SEASON!
SUDDENLY I FEEL VERY OLD...
9-8
SCHULZ

LIFE IS JUST TOO MUCH FOR ME..
I'VE BEEN CONFUSED RIGHT FROM THE DAY I WAS BORN...
9-9
I THINK THE WHOLE TROUBLE IS THAT WE'RE THROWN INTO LIFE TOO FAST...WE'RE NOT REALLY PREPARED...
WHAT DID YOU WANT...A CHANCE TO WARM UP FIRST?
SCHULZ

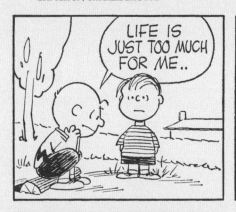

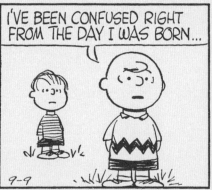

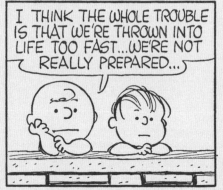

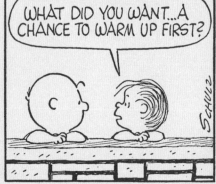

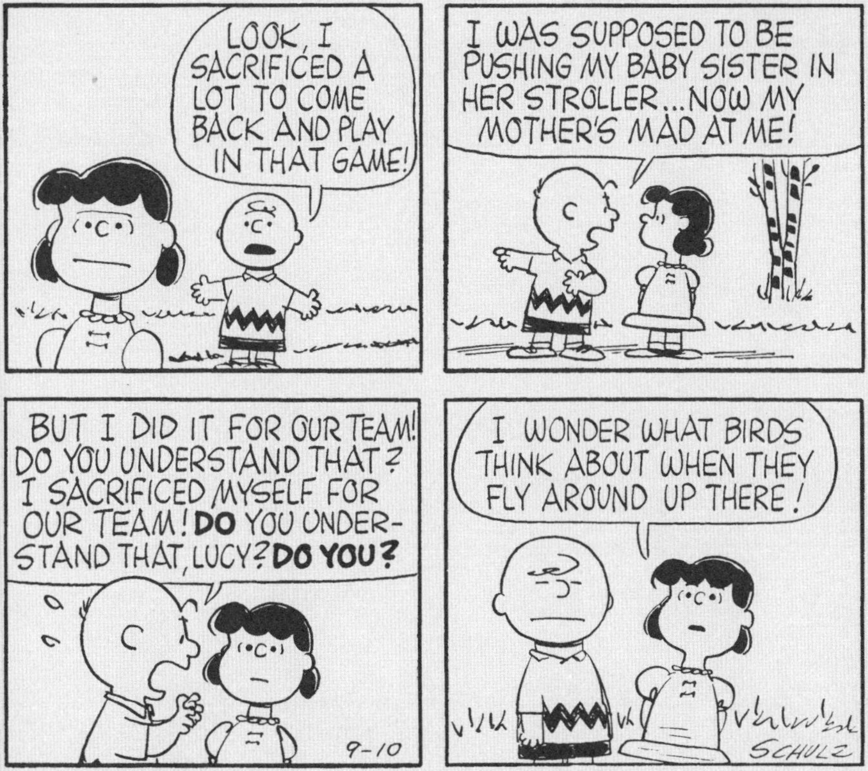
LOOK, I SACRIFICED A LOT TO COME BACK AND PLAY IN THAT GAME!
I WAS SUPPOSED TO BE PUSHING MY BABY SISTER IN HER STROLLER...NOW MY MOTHER'S MAD AT ME!
BUT I DID IT FOR OUR TEAM! DO YOU UNDERSTAND THAT? I SACRIFICED MYSELF FOR OUR TEAM! **DO** YOU UNDERSTAND THAT, LUCY? **DO YOU?**
9-10
I WONDER WHAT BIRDS THINK ABOUT WHEN THEY FLY AROUND UP THERE!
SCHULZ

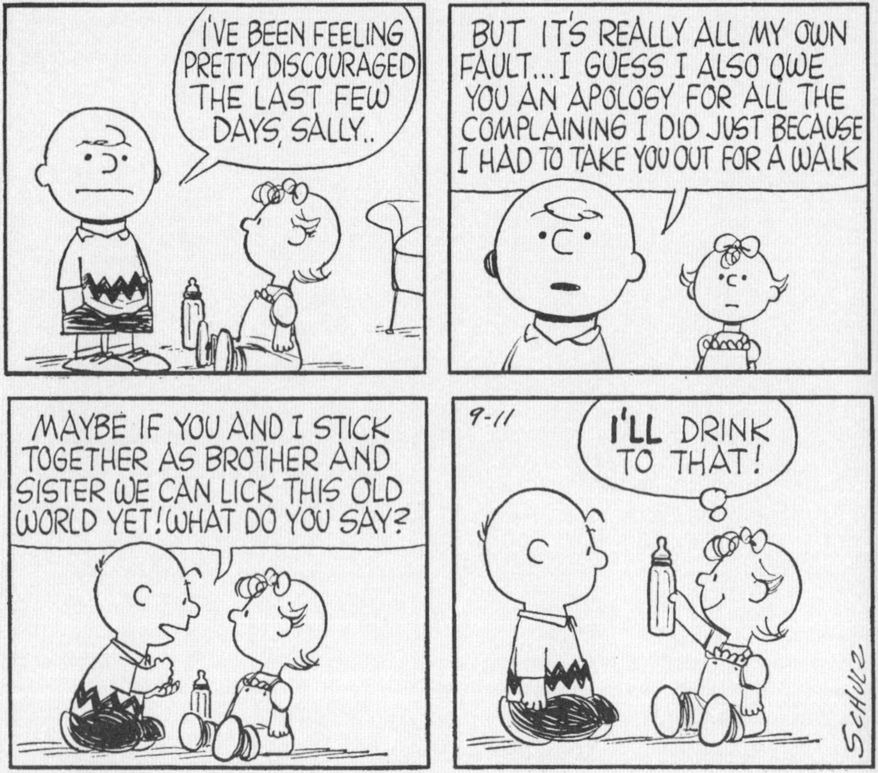
I'VE BEEN FEELING PRETTY DISCOURAGED THE LAST FEW DAYS, SALLY..
BUT IT'S REALLY ALL MY OWN FAULT... I GUESS I ALSO OWE YOU AN APOLOGY FOR ALL THE COMPLAINING I DID JUST BECAUSE I HAD TO TAKE YOU OUT FOR A WALK
MAYBE IF YOU AND I STICK TOGETHER AS BROTHER AND SISTER WE CAN LICK THIS OLD WORLD YET! WHAT DO YOU SAY?
9-11
I'LL DRINK TO THAT!
SCHULZ

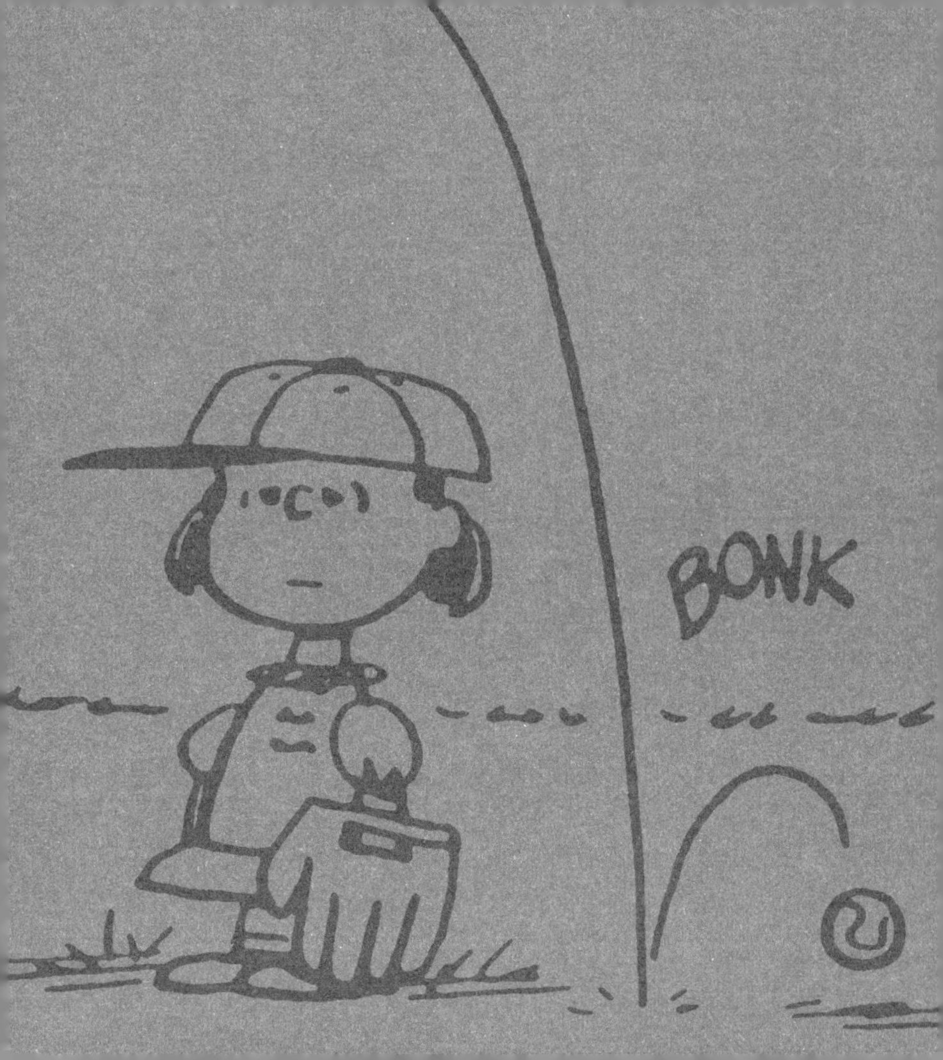
BONK

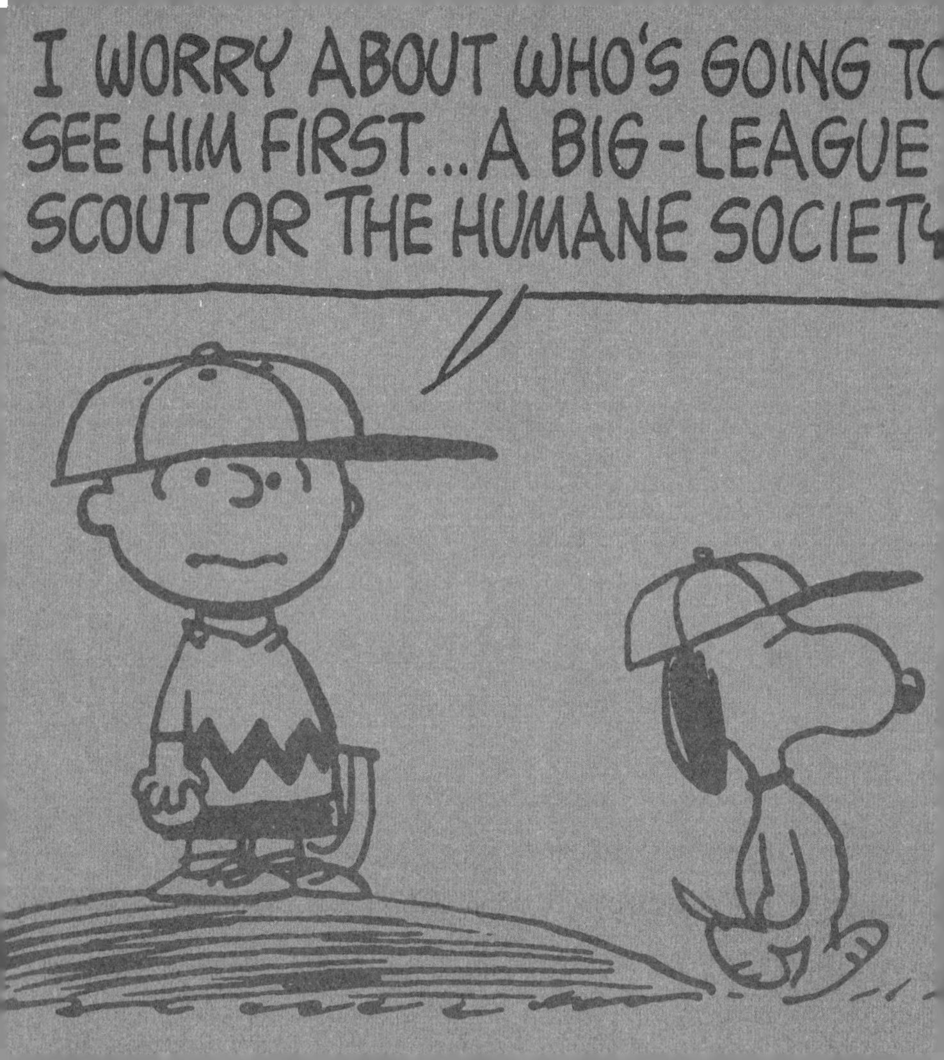
I WORRY ABOUT WHO'S GOING TO SEE HIM FIRST... A BIG-LEAGUE SCOUT OR THE HUMANE SOCIETY

XXX

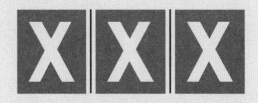

"SLIDE!"

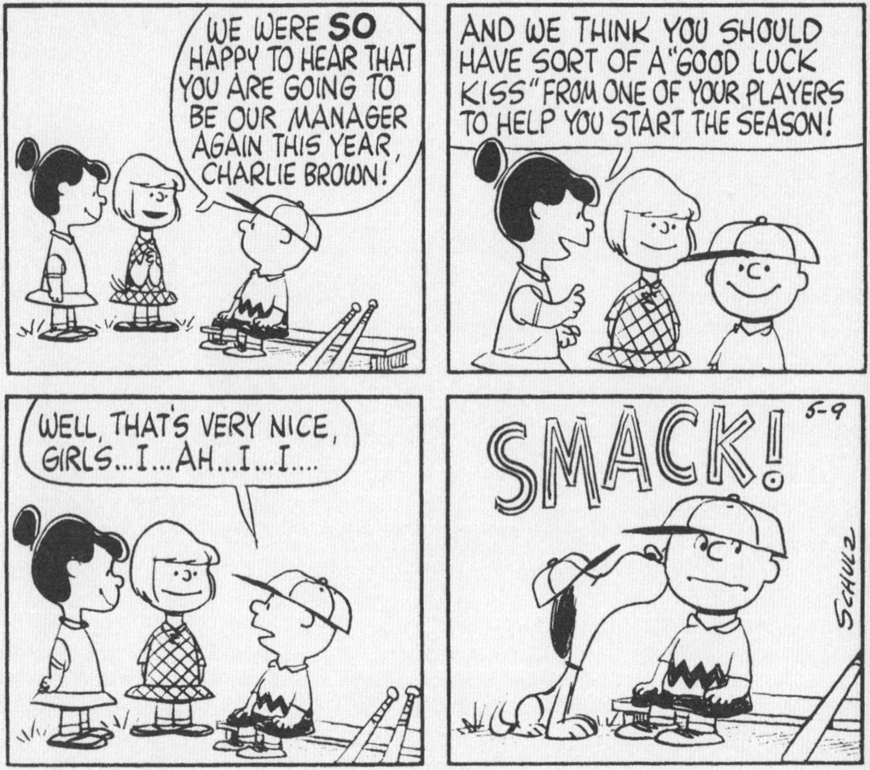
WE WERE **SO** HAPPY TO HEAR THAT YOU ARE GOING TO BE OUR MANAGER AGAIN THIS YEAR, CHARLIE BROWN!
AND WE THINK YOU SHOULD HAVE SORT OF A "GOOD LUCK KISS" FROM ONE OF YOUR PLAYERS TO HELP YOU START THE SEASON!
WELL, THAT'S VERY NICE, GIRLS...I...AH...I...I....
SMACK!
5-9
SCHULZ

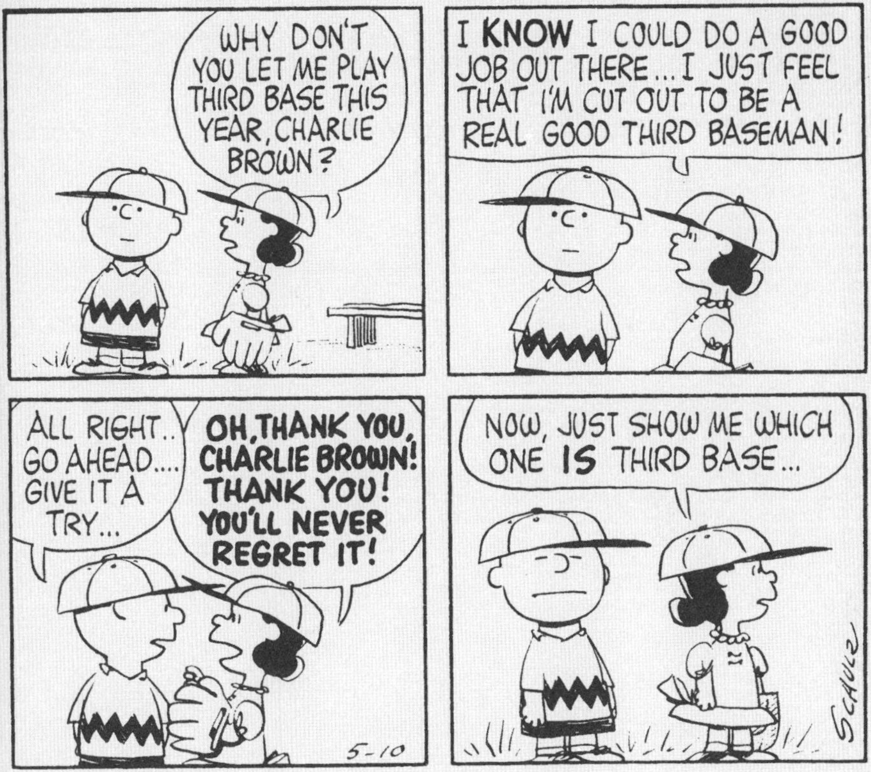
WHY DON'T YOU LET ME PLAY THIRD BASE THIS YEAR, CHARLIE BROWN?
I **KNOW** I COULD DO A GOOD JOB OUT THERE... I JUST FEEL THAT I'M CUT OUT TO BE A REAL GOOD THIRD BASEMAN!
ALL RIGHT.. GO AHEAD.... GIVE IT A TRY...
OH, THANK YOU, CHARLIE BROWN! THANK YOU! YOU'LL NEVER REGRET IT!
5-10
NOW, JUST SHOW ME WHICH ONE **IS** THIRD BASE...
SCHULZ

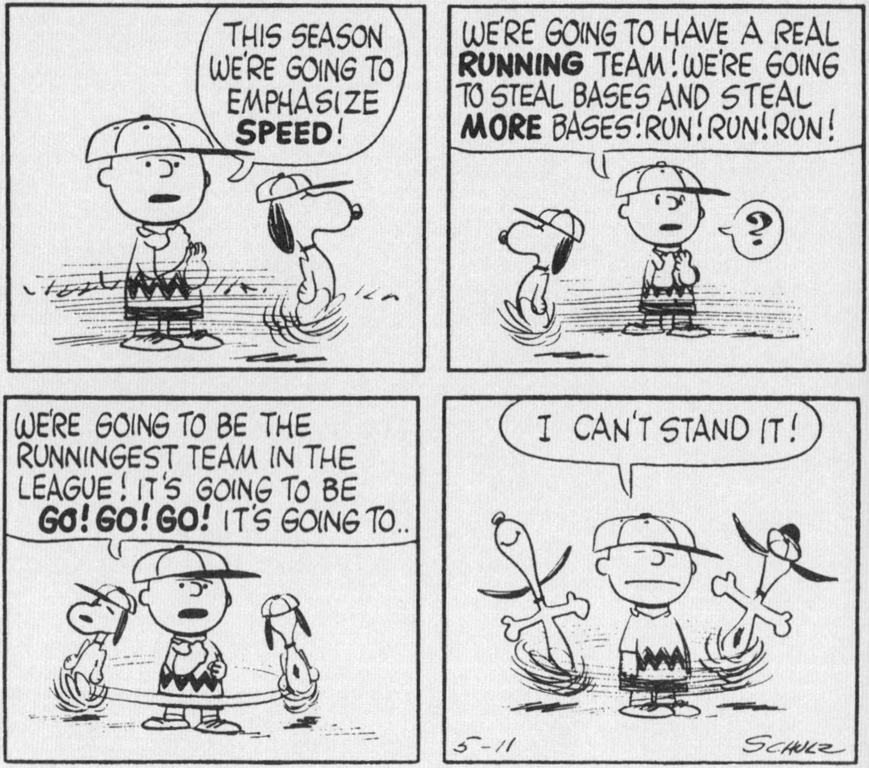
THIS SEASON WE'RE GOING TO EMPHASIZE **SPEED**!
WE'RE GOING TO HAVE A REAL **RUNNING** TEAM! WE'RE GOING TO STEAL BASES AND STEAL **MORE** BASES! RUN! RUN! RUN!
?
WE'RE GOING TO BE THE RUNNINGEST TEAM IN THE LEAGUE! IT'S GOING TO BE **GO! GO! GO!** IT'S GOING TO..
I CAN'T STAND IT!
5-11
SCHULZ

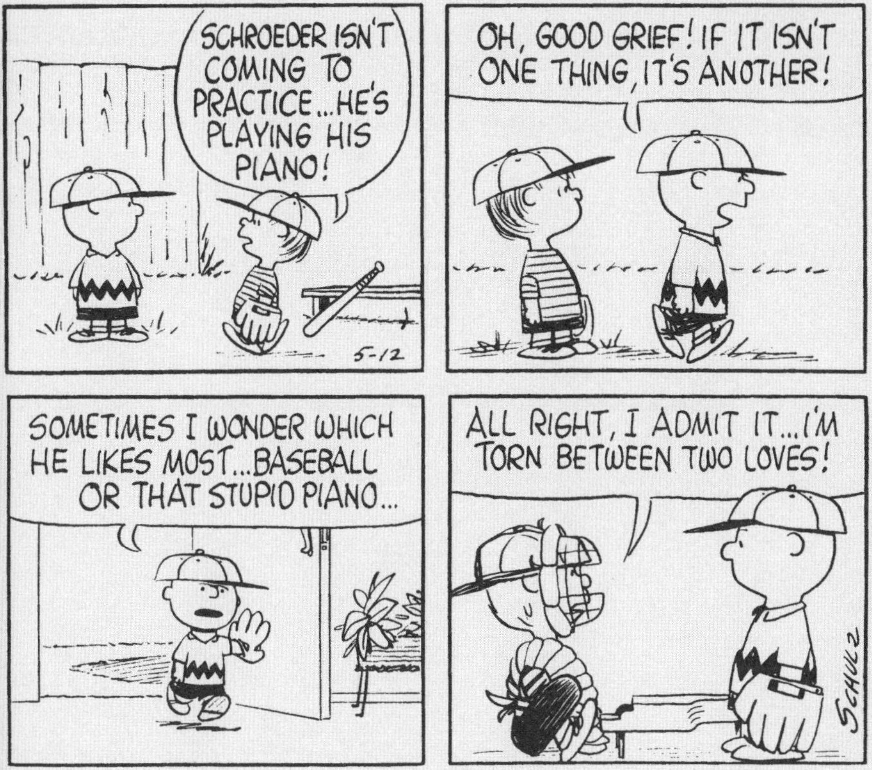
SCHROEDER ISN'T COMING TO PRACTICE...HE'S PLAYING HIS PIANO!
5-12
OH, GOOD GRIEF! IF IT ISN'T ONE THING, IT'S ANOTHER!
SOMETIMES I WONDER WHICH HE LIKES MOST...BASEBALL OR THAT STUPID PIANO...
ALL RIGHT, I ADMIT IT...I'M TORN BETWEEN TWO LOVES!
SCHULZ

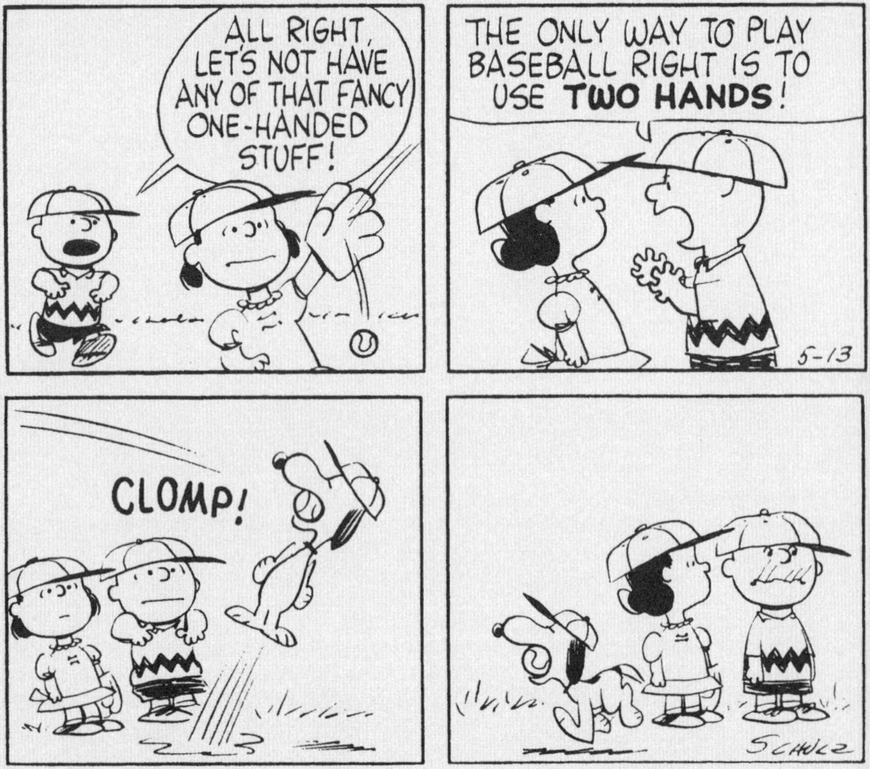
ALL RIGHT, LET'S NOT HAVE ANY OF THAT FANCY ONE-HANDED STUFF!
THE ONLY WAY TO PLAY BASEBALL RIGHT IS TO USE **TWO HANDS**!
5-13
CLOMP!
SCHULZ

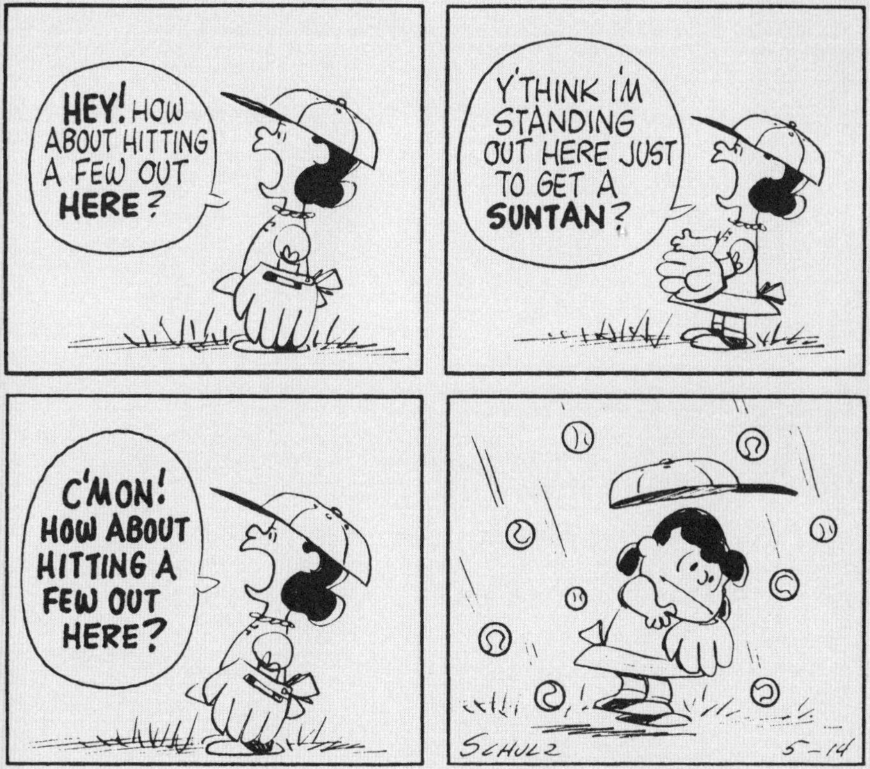
HEY! HOW ABOUT HITTING A FEW OUT HERE?
Y'THINK I'M STANDING OUT HERE JUST TO GET A SUNTAN?
C'MON! HOW ABOUT HITTING A FEW OUT HERE?
SCHULZ
5-14

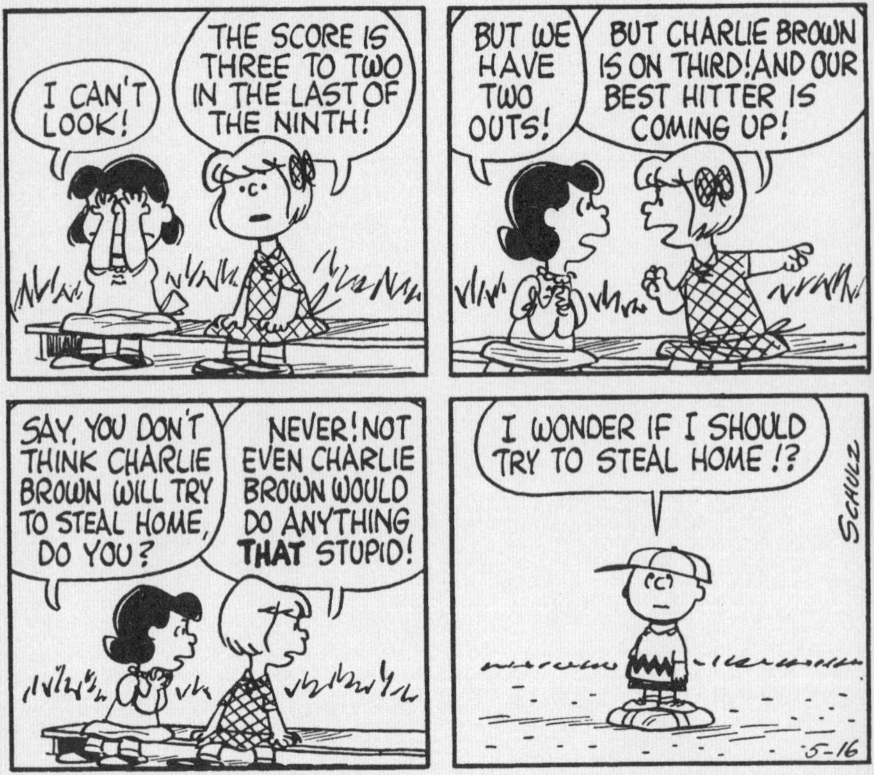
I CAN'T LOOK!
THE SCORE IS THREE TO TWO IN THE LAST OF THE NINTH!
BUT WE HAVE TWO OUTS!
BUT CHARLIE BROWN IS ON THIRD! AND OUR BEST HITTER IS COMING UP!
SAY, YOU DON'T THINK CHARLIE BROWN WILL TRY TO STEAL HOME, DO YOU?
NEVER! NOT EVEN CHARLIE BROWN WOULD DO ANYTHING THAT STUPID!
I WONDER IF I SHOULD TRY TO STEAL HOME!?
SCHULZ
5-16

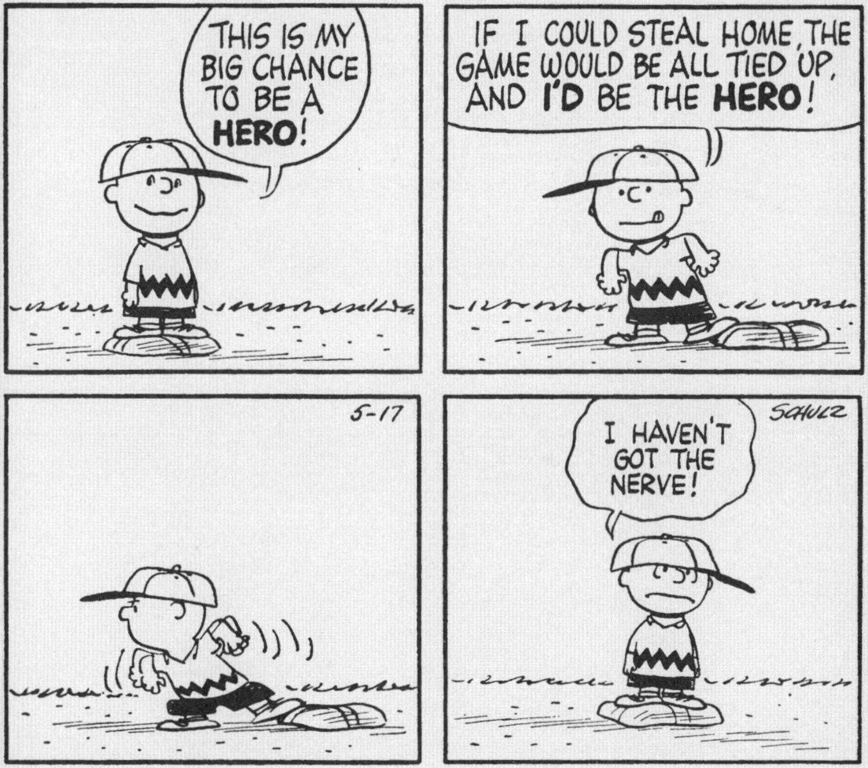
THIS IS MY BIG CHANCE TO BE A **HERO**!
IF I COULD STEAL HOME, THE GAME WOULD BE ALL TIED UP, AND **I'D** BE THE **HERO**!
5-17
SCHULZ
I HAVEN'T GOT THE NERVE!

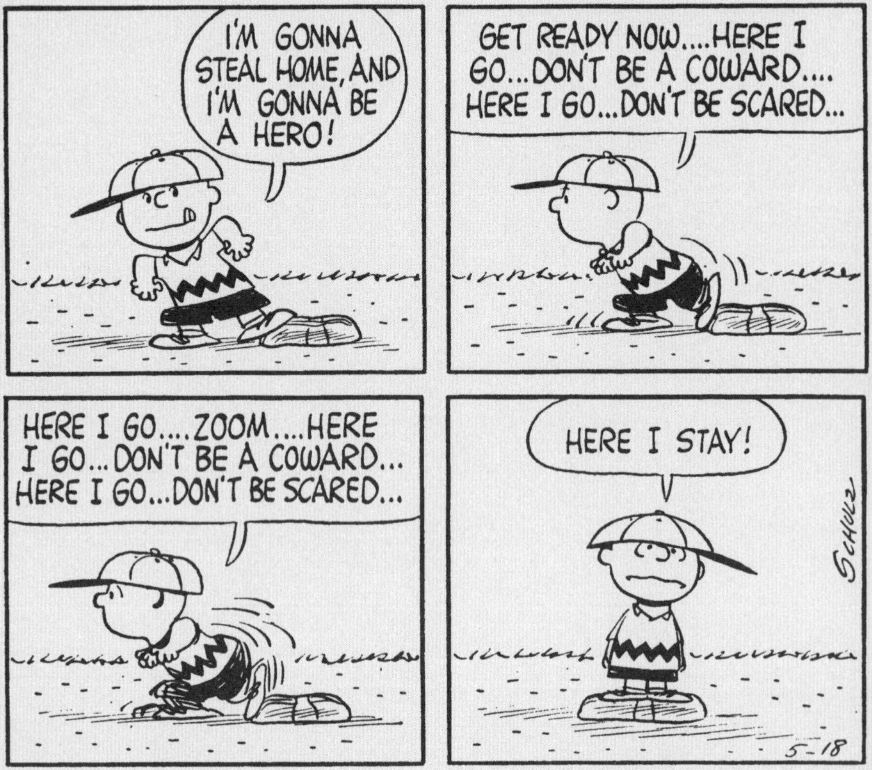
I'M GONNA STEAL HOME, AND I'M GONNA BE A HERO!
GET READY NOW....HERE I GO...DON'T BE A COWARD.... HERE I GO...DON'T BE SCARED...
HERE I GO....ZOOM....HERE I GO...DON'T BE A COWARD... HERE I GO...DON'T BE SCARED...
HERE I STAY!
SCHULZ
5-18

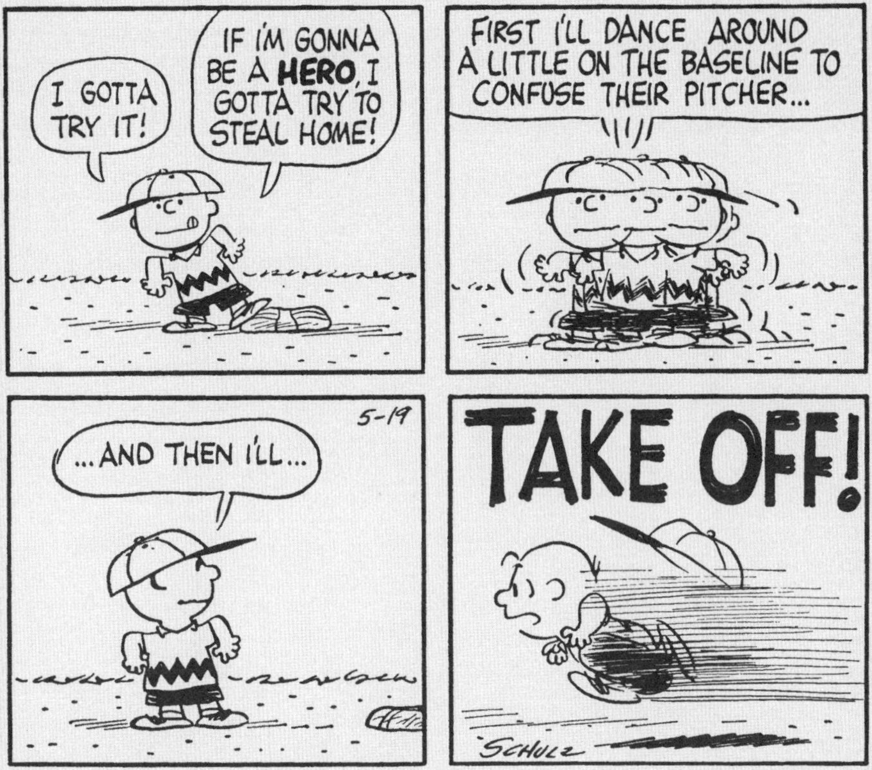
I GOTTA TRY IT!
IF I'M GONNA BE A **HERO**, I GOTTA TRY TO STEAL HOME!
FIRST I'LL DANCE AROUND A LITTLE ON THE BASELINE TO CONFUSE THEIR PITCHER...
5-19
...AND THEN I'LL...
TAKE OFF!
SCHULZ

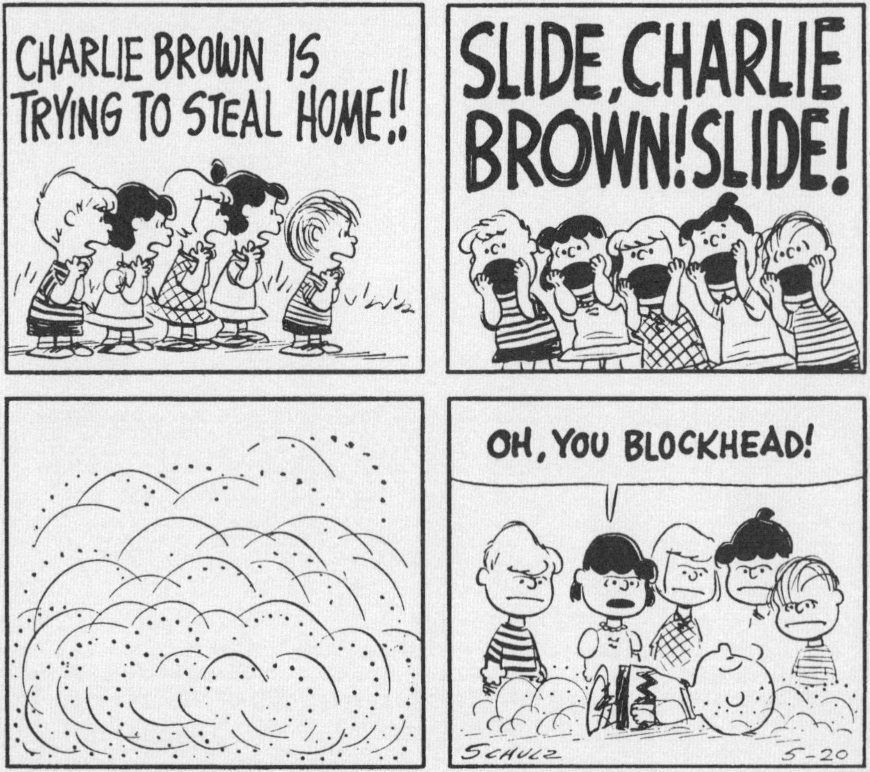
CHARLIE BROWN IS TRYING TO STEAL HOME!!
SLIDE, CHARLIE BROWN! SLIDE!
OH, YOU BLOCKHEAD!
SCHULZ
5-20

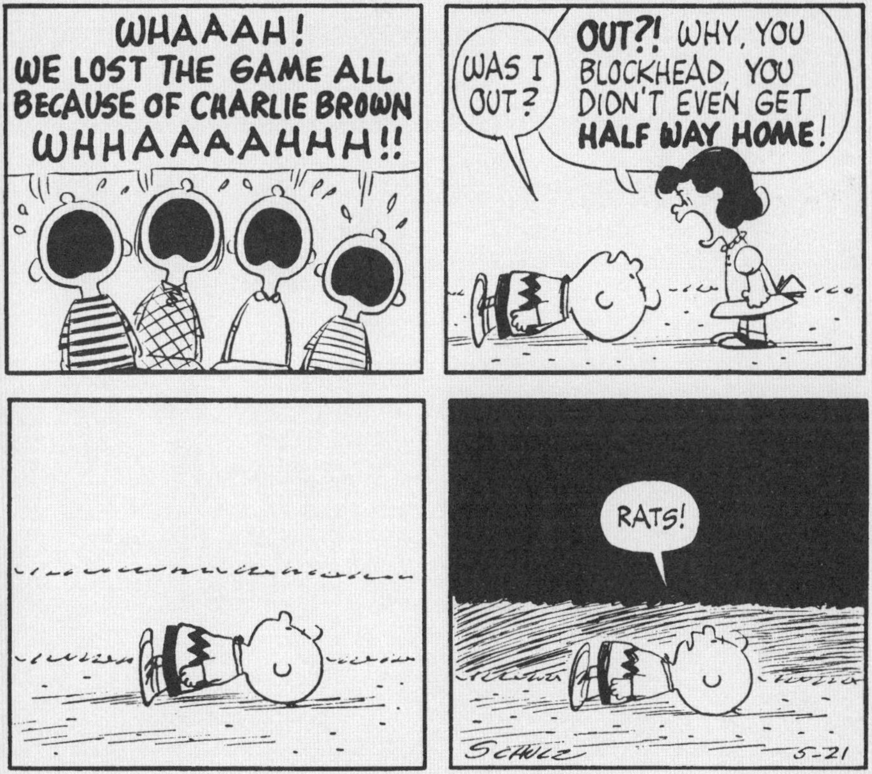
WHAAAH!
WE LOST THE GAME ALL BECAUSE OF CHARLIE BROWN
WHHAAAAAHHH!!
WAS I OUT?
OUT?! WHY, YOU BLOCKHEAD, YOU DIDN'T EVEN GET HALF WAY HOME!
RATS!
SCHULZ
5-21

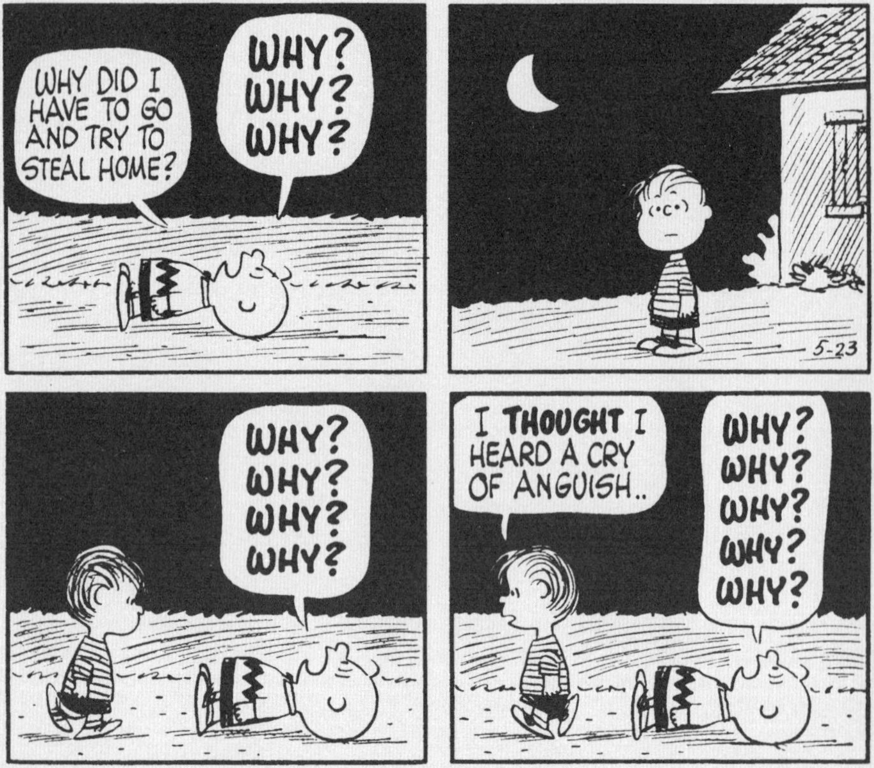
WHY DID I HAVE TO GO AND TRY TO STEAL HOME?
WHY? WHY? WHY?
5-23
WHY? WHY? WHY? WHY?
I THOUGHT I HEARD A CRY OF ANGUISH..
WHY? WHY? WHY? WHY? WHY?

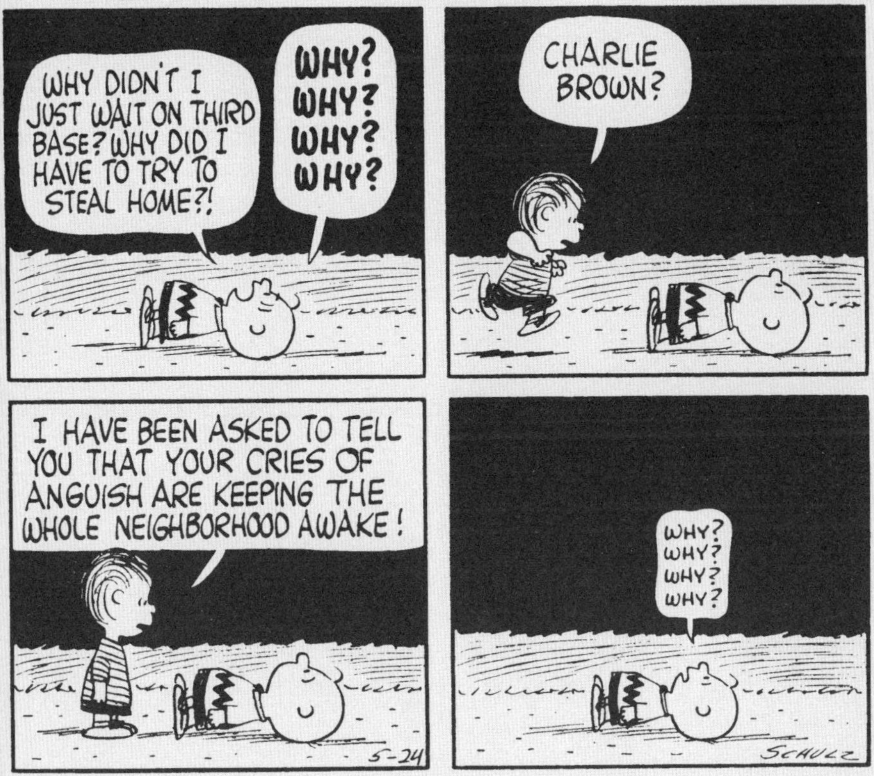
WHY DIDN'T I JUST WAIT ON THIRD BASE? WHY DID I HAVE TO TRY TO STEAL HOME?!
WHY? WHY? WHY? WHY?
CHARLIE BROWN?
I HAVE BEEN ASKED TO TELL YOU THAT YOUR CRIES OF ANGUISH ARE KEEPING THE WHOLE NEIGHBORHOOD AWAKE!
5-24
WHY? WHY? WHY? WHY?
SCHULZ

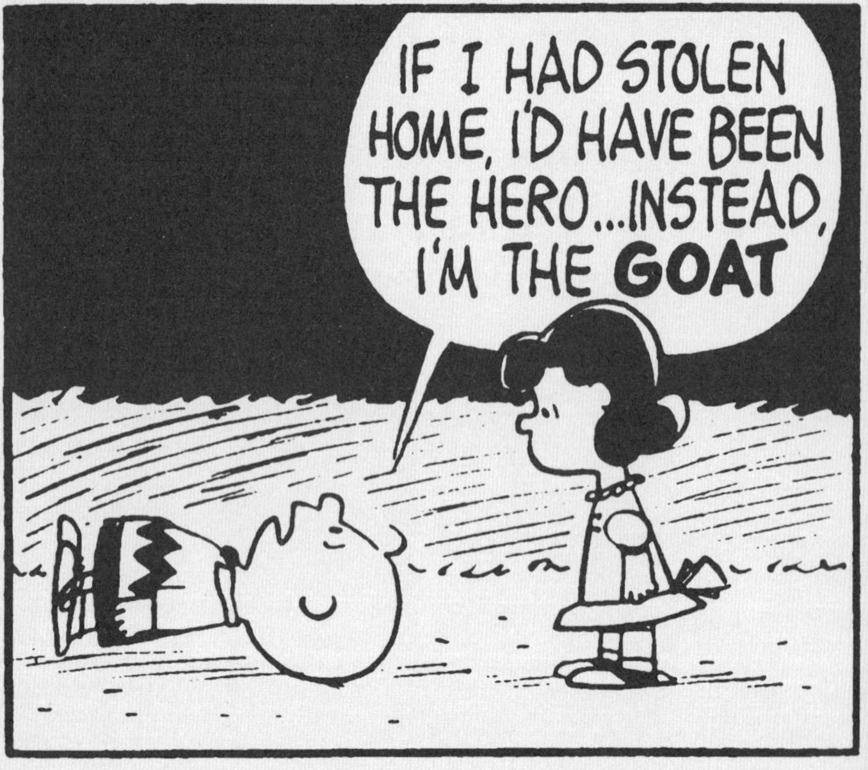
IF I HAD STOLEN HOME, I'D HAVE BEEN THE HERO...INSTEAD, I'M THE GOAT

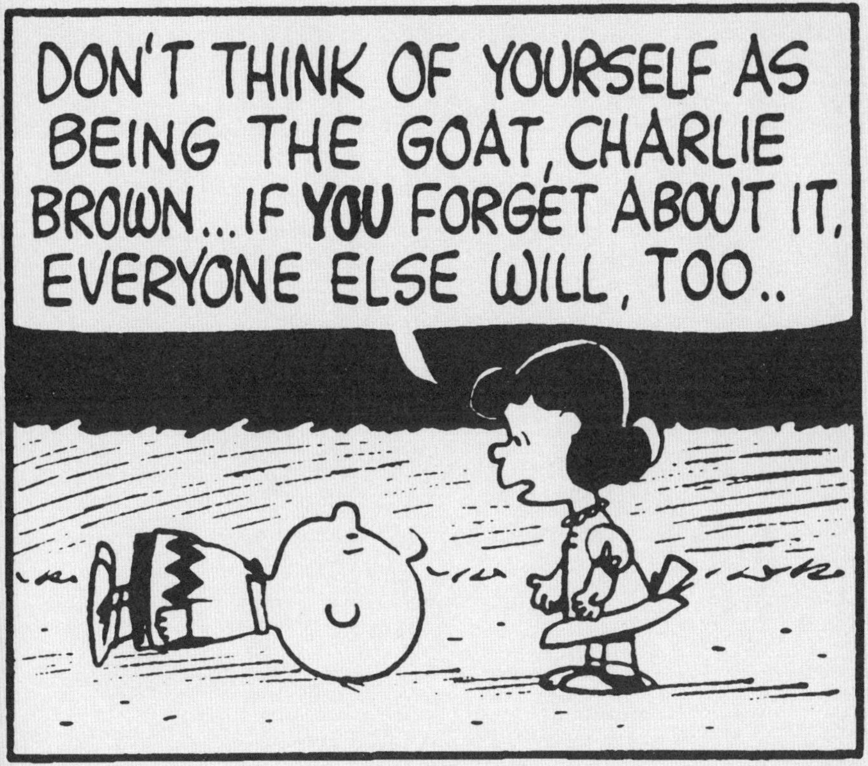
DON'T THINK OF YOURSELF AS BEING THE GOAT, CHARLIE BROWN... IF **YOU** FORGET ABOUT IT, EVERYONE ELSE WILL, TOO..

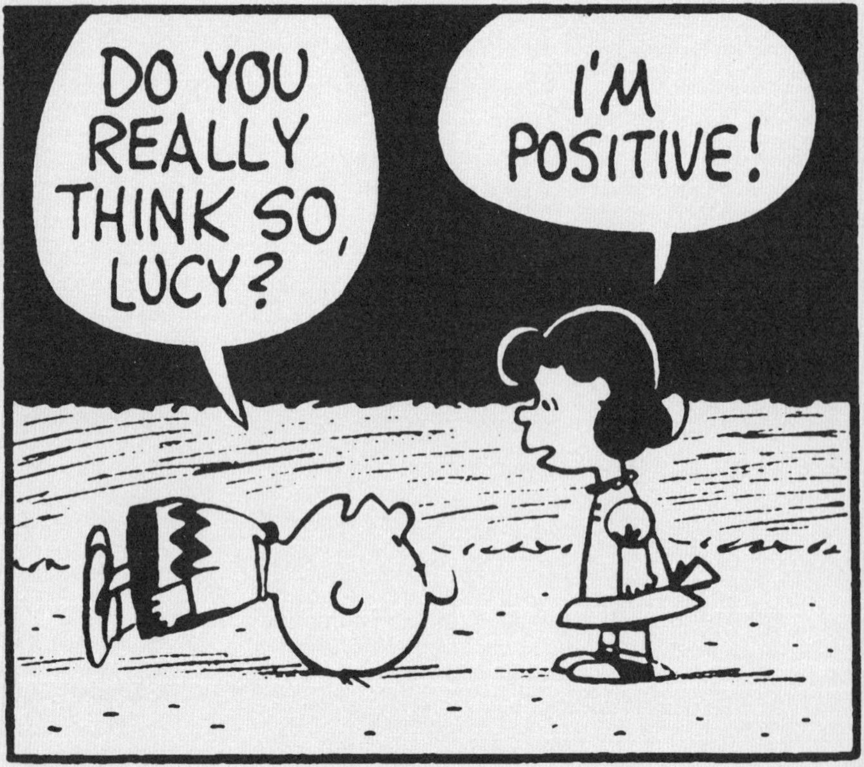
DO YOU REALLY THINK SO, LUCY?
I'M POSITIVE!

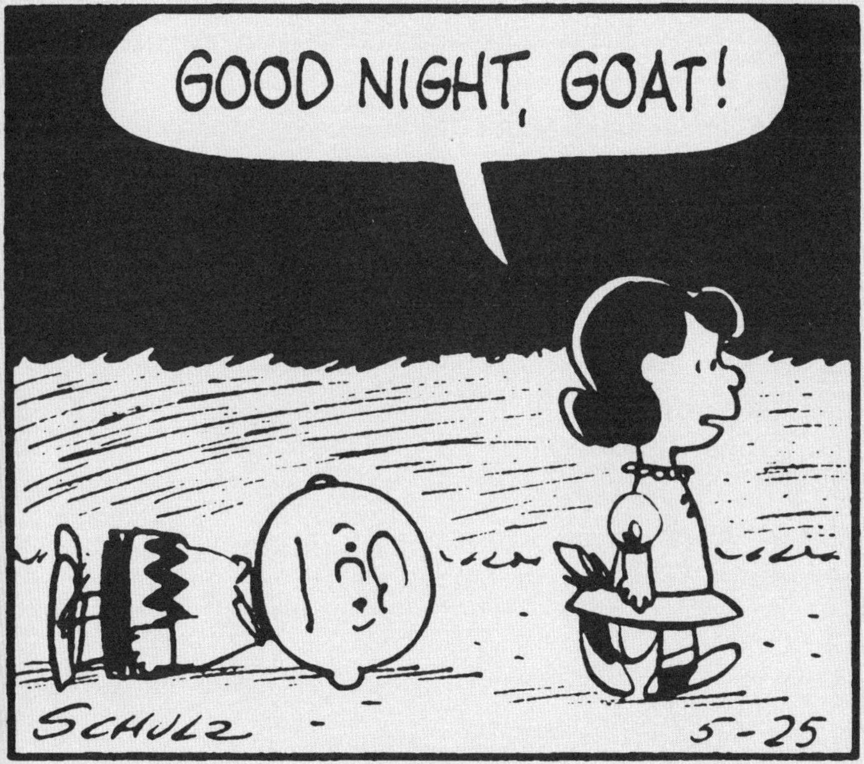
GOOD NIGHT, GOAT!
SCHULZ
5-25

Editor: GARY GROTH
Designer: JACOB COVEY
Associate Publisher: ERIC REYNOLDS
Publisher: GARY GROTH

FANTAGRAPHICS BOOKS, 7563 Lake City Way, Seattle, WA 98115, USA.
For a free full-color catalogue of comics, call 1-800-657-1100.
Our books may be viewed on our website at www.fantagraphics.com.

Special thanks to Marcie Daniel.

Thanks also to Secret Headquarters, John DiBello, Karen Green, Eduardo Takeo "Lizarkeo" Igarashi, Ted Haycraft, Andy Koopmans, Juan Manuel Domínguez, Paul van Dijken, Nick Capetillo, Randall Bethune, Kevin Czapiewski, Thomas Eykemans, Christian Schremser, Thomas Zimmermann, Kurt Sayenga, Anne Lise Rostgaard Schmidt, Coco and Eddie Gorodetsky, Big Planet Comics, Nevdon Jamgochian, Dan Evans III, Scott Fritsch-Hammes, Black Hook Press, Mungo van Krimpen-Hall, Jason Aaron Way, Vanessa Palacios, Mathieu Doublet, and Philip Nel

ISBN: 978-1-60699-725-3 . First printing: April, 2014 . Printed in China

FANTAGRAPHICS BOOKS

HOW CAN WE LOSE WHEN WE'RE SO SINCERE ?!

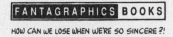